GALÁPAGOS ISLANDS

BEN WESTWOOD

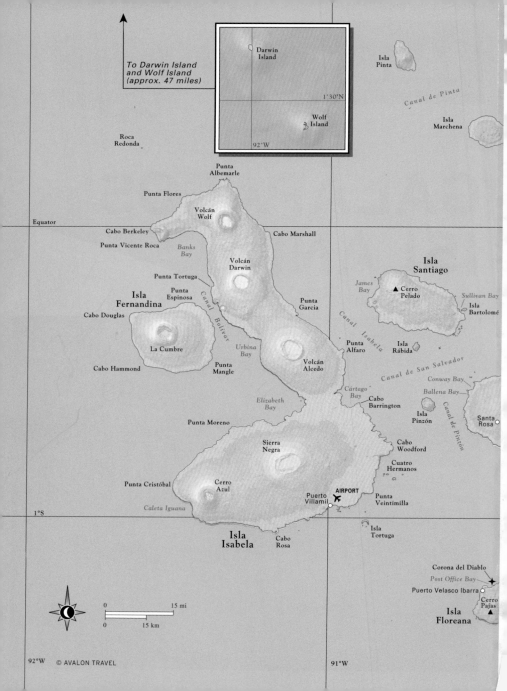

GALÁPAGOS ISLANDS

Equator

GALÁPAGOS ISLANDS

MEX · BLZ · HND · GTM · SLV · NIC · HTI · DOM · CRI · PAN · VEN · COL · ECU · BRA · PER · BOL

PACIFIC OCEAN

| 0 | 500 mi |
| 0 | 500 km |

PACIFIC OCEAN

Isla Genovesa

Darwin Bay

Canal de Marchena

Galápagos Islands National Park

Isla Seymour Norte

Isla Baltra

Isla Daphne

✈ AIRPORT

Gordon Rocks

Plaza Sur

Cerro Crocker ▲

Isla Santa Cruz

Bellavista

Puerto Ayora

Tortuga Bay

Canal de Santa Cruz

Isla Santa Fé

Canal de Santa Fé

Isla San Cristóbal

Kicker Rock

Esteban Bay

Isla Lobos

Punta Pitt

Rosa Blanca Bay

AIRPORT ✈ El Progreso

PUERTO BAQUERIZO MORENO

Hancock Bank

McGowen Reef

Punta Ayora

Caldwell

Gardner

Gardner

Gardner Bay

Punta Suárez

Isla Española

90°W

89°W

Contents

Discover the Galápagos Islands

The Galápagos is one place on earth that lives up to and surpasses expectations. There are insufficient superlatives. This archipelago is unquestionably the best place on earth for wildlife watching because the wildlife watches you as much as you watch it. The lack of natural predators has left the animals fearless, and the only timid species are the fish, the food supply for so many. Every other creature on the islands is either unconcerned by the presence of visitors or is intent on communicating.

The Galápagos is also heaven for bird-watchers. Here you don't need to get up at dawn and wait with binoculars for a glimpse of birdlife in the trees. Instead, the birds proudly display themselves – the male frigates inflate their red chests to the size of a basketball, the albatross entertain with their circular clacking dance, and pelicans dive-bomb the ocean in search of lunch.

A visit to these islands changes you, as it changed Charles Darwin, who was inspired to form his monumental theory of evolution after visiting in 1835. The Galápagos is a glimpse of what life was like before humans threw their weight around, and a reminder that when we seek out perfection, we throw a wrench in nature's works. Evidence of human activity on the Galápagos is everywhere – the number of endemic species hunted or driven to near extinction by introduced species is alarming. But the effort of conservationists to restore the ecological balance is equally inspiring. You will return from these islands filled with a sense of wonder, and a clearer view of nature's fragile beauty.

Planning Your Trip

▶ WHERE TO GO

Santa Cruz and Nearby Islands

The archipelago's tourism hub is centered around the busy but pleasant Puerto Ayora. Highlights include the Charles Darwin Research Station and Tortuga Bay, one of the islands' most beautiful beaches. Lava tunnels, craters, and lush hills await in the highlands, while surrounding islands provide excellent excursions, notably the sea lion colony on Plaza Sur, and frigates and blue-footed boobies on Seymour Norte.

San Cristóbal

Sea lions dominate the waterfront of Puerto Baquerizo Moreno, and you can walk among a large colony close to town at La Lobería. Offshore, the trip to Isla Lobos and Kicker Rock offers unrivalled snorkeling with sea lions and sharks. Inland is the huge giant tortoise reserve La Galapaguera, and at the far

east side of the island is Punta Pitt, one of the few spots where all three booby species are seen together.

Santiago and Nearby Islands

The blackened lava trails of Santiago recall a land that time forgot. Explore this unworldly landscape in the trails around Sullivan Bay. The nearby islet of Bartolomé—a partially eroded lava formation flanked by two beaches with the black lava trails of Santiago in the distance—is the most photographed sight in the Galápagos.

Western Islands

Isabela is the giant of the archipelago, occupying half the total land mass. It also boasts the most dramatic landscapes, with six active volcanoes. The highlight is the Sierra Negra hike around the second largest crater

sea lion on Santa Fé, just south of Santa Cruz

red-footed booby on Genovesa

black lava trails on Bartolomé

flamingo at Punta Cormorant

in the world before descending into the sulfur mines. Fernandina is one of the least visited islands, and Punta Espinosa, the sole visitor site, has the largest colony of marine iguanas in the archipelago and the biggest nesting site for flightless cormorants.

Southern Islands

Floreana's lush, peaceful ambience belies its troubled history, which has kept amateur sleuths guessing for decades. Highlights include a quirky post office, excellent snorkeling at Devil's Crown, and flocks of flamingos at Punta Cormorant. Española is the world's biggest breeding site in the world for waved albatross.

Northern Islands

Fewer boats make it to the far north, but Genovesa is enduringly popular for its large red-footed booby populations. Wolf and Darwin Islands are the preserve of experienced divers who can enjoy the awe-inspiring sight of whale sharks from June to November.

▶ WHEN TO GO

Although the Galápagos is a year-round destination, the best conditions are December to April. The seas are calmer, the weather mostly sunny and hot, and rain on the larger islands leads to an explosion of greenery. This coincides with the busiest tourist period at Christmas, Carnival (usually February), and Easter. From June to October the weather is cooler, so it's more comfortable on land, but the landscapes are more barren and the sea becomes rougher, so seasickness is more of a problem. The waters can be surprisingly cold for swimming and snorkeling, but on the positive side, the cooler temperatures sometimes bring higher numbers of marine creatures to watch. The islands have short low-seasons in May–June and September–October, either side of the July–August high season. These are the best times to secure last-minute availability, although September is often used by cruise-boat owners as an opportunity to do annual maintenance work. However, cut-price deals can be found year-round if you look hard enough and are flexible.

► BEFORE YOU GO

Passports, Tourist Cards, and Visas

Travelers to Ecuador will need a passport that is valid for at least six months beyond the date of entry. A tourist card (also called a T-3) is issued on entry and must be returned on leaving Ecuador. Stays of up to 90 days are permitted without a visa and can sometimes be extended a further 90 days in mainland Ecuador. Travelers must also be able to show "proof of economic means" (a credit card is usually good enough) and a return or onward travel ticket out of Ecuador.

To enter the Galápagos, you must obtain the mandatory $10 transit control card from your departure airport (either Quito or Guayaquil). This helps to regulate the exact number of visitors. Upon arrival in the archipelago there is a mandatory $100 national park entrance fee, payable in cash. It's a hefty fee, but it helps to preserve the islands' fragile ecosystem. If you have a student or cultural visa, you pay $25, while Ecuadorians pay just $6. Note that a recent crackdown on illegal immigration means that staying beyond 90 days will result in immediate deportation.

Vaccinations

All visitors should make sure their routine immunizations are up to date. The U.S. Centers for Disease Control and Prevention recommend that travelers be vaccinated against hepatitis A, typhoid fever, and in cases of close contact with locals, hepatitis B. Rabies vaccinations are also recommended for those venturing into rural areas. Proof of yellow fever vaccination is necessary when entering Ecuador from Peru or Colombia, but it is a good idea no matter where you arrive from. Note that there have been some cases of Dengue fever on the Galápagos recently. There is no vaccine, so wear long, light-colored clothing and use mosquito repellent.

Photographers take pictures of sea lions on Española Island.

a row of traditional Ecuadorian dolls at a handicrafts store on the Galápagos Islands

Booking a Tour

In simple terms, the farther you are from the Galápagos, the more you pay. Cruises, land tours, and diving tours can all be arranged in your home country or through a travel agency in Ecuador. Keep in mind that when booking a tour from abroad a deposit of at least $200 per person, via wire transfer or Western Union (no credit cards by Internet or phone), is usually required.

Many travel agencies in Quito and Guayaquil advertise tours, so shopping around is the way to go. Holding out for last-minute deals may save you anywhere from 5 to 35 percent, but be aware that it may leave you stranded as well. Some travelers with time on their hands even fly to the Galápagos, book into a cheap hotel for a few days, and take their chances on finding a last-minute cruise, saving 50 percent in some cases; but there are no guarantees.

Transportation

Transportation to the islands is generally not included in the price of a tour. Flights to the Galápagos depart from Quito and Guayaquil daily. There are two entrance airports in the Galápagos: one on Baltra, just north of the central island of Santa Cruz, and one on San Cristóbal. The airport on Isabela is only used for interisland flights. Make sure you're flying to the correct island to begin your tour. Prices are about $350 round-trip from Guayaquil and $400 from Quito.

If you are traveling to the islands without being booked on a tour, Puerto Ayora is the best place to arrange a budget tour. Note that getting from Baltra to Puerto Ayora is a journey in three stages involving two bus rides and a ferry ride. There are daily ferry shuttles from $25 per person one-way to the other two main ports—Baquerizo Moreno on San Cristóbal and Puerto Villamil on Isabela.

Explore the Galápagos Islands

▶ CRUISE TOURS

Tour boats are organized into five classes—economy, tourist, tourist superior, first, and luxury. Economy-class boats are very basic and appropriate for those on a very limited budget or time frame; tourist- and tourist superior-class boats are the most common in the islands, with a bit more comfort and better guides; first class and luxury tours offer air-conditioning, gourmet food, and service that matches those in the finest hotels on the mainland, and guides are qualified scientists. Prices vary widely, but all prices should include food, accommodations, transfers to and from your boat, trained guides, and all your shore visits.

A good guide is the most important factor in your visit. All Galápagos guides are trained and licensed by the National Park Service and qualify in one of three classes, in ascending order of quality. When booking a tour, ask about your guide's specific qualifications and what language(s) he or she speaks.

SAMPLE ITINERARIES

A tour of at least five days is recommended, and seven or eight days is even better, as it takes half a day each way to get to and from the islands. Most travelers visit the isles on packaged tours, but it's increasingly easy to do it yourself, stay in the three main ports, take day trips, and shuttle between islands.

There are basically three itineraries: northern, southern, and western. Five-day tours include one of these areas, and eight-day tours include two; it's only possible to experience all three areas on the more expensive and rarer two-week tours. Note that the western itinerary has fewer departures and is mainly

A tour on *La Pinta* guarantees guests the best level of cruise comfort available on the Galápagos Islands.

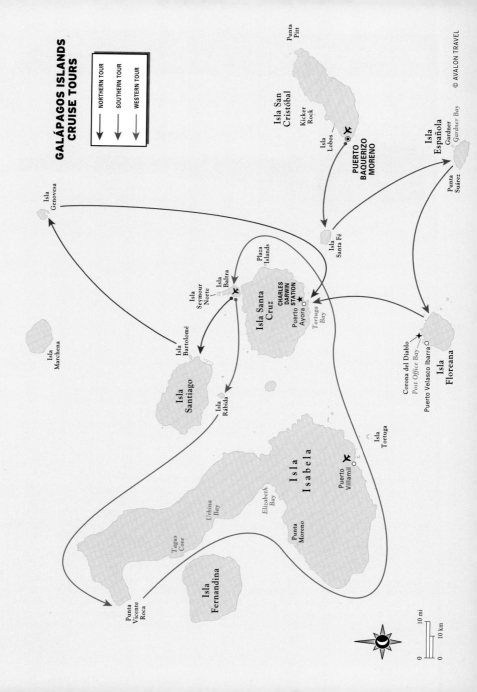

GALÁPAGOS ISLANDS CRUISE TOURS

→ NORTHERN TOUR
→ SOUTHERN TOUR
→ WESTERN TOUR

Punta Pitt

Isla San Cristóbal

Kicker Rock

Isla Lobos

PUERTO BAQUERIZO MORENO

Isla Genovesa

Isla Santa Fé

Plaza Islands

Isla Baltra

Isla Seymour Norte

Isla Santa Cruz

CHARLES DARWIN STATION
Puerto Ayora
Tortuga Bay

Isla Marchena

Isla Bartolomé

Isla Santiago

Isla Rábida

Corona del Diablo
Post Office Bay
Puerto Velasco Ibarra

Isla Floreana

Isla Española

Gardner
Gardner Bay

Punta Suárez

Isla Tortuga

Isla Isabela

Puerto Villamil

Urbina Bay

Elizabeth Bay

Punta Moreno

Tagus Cove

Isla Fernandina

Punta Vicente Roca

0   10 mi
0   10 km

© AVALON TRAVEL

BEST BEACHES

Tortuga Bay

Most travelers don't come to the Galápagos to lie on beaches but rather to watch animals lying on beaches. However, many of the visitor sites are located around beautiful sandy stretches, and you may welcome the chance to sun yourself like a lazy iguana after a hard day of watching wildlife.

Tortuga Bay, Santa Cruz (p. 60)
The longest beach in the archipelago is a 45-minute walk from Puerto Ayora on Santa Cruz. The first beach has strong currents and is popular with surfers, but walk to the end and soak in a sheltered shallow lagoon at Playa Mansa, where marine turtles lay eggs at night.

Bachas Beach, Santa Cruz (p. 62)
This beach is named for the remains of wrecked U.S. military barges from World War II, and the rusty metal parts remain visible, jutting out of the white sand. The beach is otherwise pristine and covered in sally lightfoot crabs, while the lagoons behind are home to flamingos.

Puerto Chino, San Cristóbal (p. 71)
San Cristóbal has many beautiful beaches – Playa del Amor, La Lobería, and Cerro Brujo – but this beach is one of the quietest. Used as a cool-off after a trip to the highlands, the small beach is backed by mangroves and is also good for surfing.

Puerto Villamil, Isabela (p. 76)
The main port on Isabela is the most laid-back town in the archipelago, with a peaceful position on a long white-sand beach that is home to a small colony of marine iguanas. Far quieter than other resorts, you may find it difficult to leave.

Post Office Bay, Floreana (p. 83)
This brown-sand beach is hardly the most photogenic in the islands, but the history behind it is interesting. The post office barrel has been running since 1793, so leave a postcard and pick up any mail for your local area. A visit is usually combined with the green-tinged beach of nearby Punta Cormorant, colored by olivine minerals.

Kicker Rock, San Cristóbal

available on eight-day tours because distances are greater. Most tours start off in Santa Cruz, but you can also start in San Cristóbal. Always check the exact itinerary and the class of boat before booking.

FIVE-DAY NORTHERN CRUISE

- Day 1: Baltra airport, Bachas Beach
- Day 2: Bartolomé, Santiago, and Rábida
- Day 3: Genovesa
- Day 4: Plaza Islands, Santa Cruz (Charles Darwin Research Station, Tortuga Bay)
- Day 5: Baltra

FIVE-DAY SOUTHERN CRUISE

- Day 1: San Cristóbal (Isla Lobos, Kicker Rock)
- Day 2: Plaza Islands, Santa Fé
- Day 3: Española (Punta Suárez, Gardner Bay)
- Day 4: Floreana (Post Office Bay, Punta Cormorant, Devil's Crown)

- Day 5: Santa Cruz (Charles Darwin Research Station), Baltra

SIX-DAY WESTERN CRUISE

- Day 1: Baltra, Rábida
- Day 2: Isabela (Punta Vicente Roca), Fernandina (Punta Espinosa)
- Day 3: Isabela (Tagus Cove, Urbina Bay)
- Day 4: Isabela (Elizabeth Bay, Punta Moreno)
- Day 5: Isabela (Puerto Villamil)
- Day 6: Seymour Norte, Baltra

EIGHT-DAY SOUTHERN AND NORTHERN CRUISE

- Day 1: San Cristóbal (Isla Lobos, Kicker Rock)
- Day 2: San Cristóbal (highlands, Punta Pitt)
- Day 3: Floreana (Post Office Bay, Punta Cormorant, Devil's Crown)

Charles Darwin Research Station

- Day 4: Santa Cruz (Black Turtle Cove), Bartolomé
- Day 5: Genovesa
- Day 6: Santiago
- Day 7: Plaza Islands, Santa Cruz (Charles Darwin Research Station)
- Day 8: Baltra

EIGHT-DAY WESTERN AND SOUTHERN CRUISE

- Day 1: Baltra, Rábida

- Day 2: Isabela (Punta Vicente Roca), Fernandina (Punta Espinosa)
- Day 3: Isabela (Tagus Cove, Urbina Bay)
- Day 4: Isabela (Elizabeth Bay, Punta Moreno)
- Day 5: Isabela (Wetlands, Wall of Tears, Tortoise Breeding Center)
- Day 6: Seymour Norte, Santa Cruz (Charles Darwin Station)
- Day 7: Española (Punta Suárez, Gardner Bay)
- Day 8: San Cristóbal (Interpretation Center, La Galapaguera)

▶ LAND TOURS

Land tours are increasingly common and are especially popular with those who suffer from seasickness. There is more flexibility in some ways, but many of the islands (for example Fernandina, Española, and Genovesa) are excluded from land-based itineraries, and many of the best sites on other islands are also excluded. Precious time is also spent traveling to and from sites every day.

SAMPLE ITINERARIES

Land tours restrict you to sites within a day's travel of three populated areas: Puerto Ayora on Santa Cruz, Baquerizo Moreno on San Cristóbal, and Puerto Villamil on Isabela. A five-day land-based tour can take in two of these islands, while an eight-day tour can take in all three plus a few day trips to nearby islands such as Seymour

Seymour Norte

Norte, Plaza Islands, Floreana, Santa Fé, and Bartolomé. Other islands are strictly off-limits to day trips.

FIVE DAYS

- Day 1: San Cristóbal (Isla Lobos, Kicker Rock)
- Day 2: Ferry to Santa Cruz (Charles Darwin Research Station, Tortuga Bay, highlands)
- Day 3: Day trip to Bartolomé
- Day 4: Day trip to Floreana, Plaza Islands, or Seymour Norte
- Day 5: Bus to Baltra

EIGHT DAYS

- Day 1: San Cristóbal (Isla Lobos, Kicker Rock)
- Day 2: Ferry to Santa Cruz (Charles Darwin Research Station), ferry to Isabela
- Day 3: Isabela (Sierra Negra trek)
- Day 4: Isabela (Las Tintoreras, Tortoise Breeding Center, Wall of Tears)
- Day 5: Ferry to Santa Cruz (highlands, Tortuga Bay)
- Day 6: Day trip to Bartolomé
- Day 7: Day trip to Floreana, Plaza Islands, or Seymour Norte
- Day 8: Bus to Baltra

flamingos on the beach on Isabela

Wildlife Guide

The Galápagos is teeming with wildlife, with around 5,000 species. The following are the major highlights of the vast wildlife-viewing opportunities in the archipelago. For more in-depth information on the natural world in the Galápagos, see page 95.

Giant Tortoises

Of the 20 species of endemic reptiles, these slow giants are the most famous. They also gave the islands their name—*galápago* is an old Spanish word for a saddle similar in shape to the tortoise shell. They are only found on the Galápagos and in smaller numbers on a few islands in the Indian Ocean.

The shell of a giant tortoise reveals which island its owner originates from. Saddle-shaped shells evolved on low, arid islands where tortoises needed to lift their heads high to eat tall vegetation, while semicircular domed shells come from higher, lush islands where vegetation grows closer to the ground.

Of the original 14 subspecies, 10 remain, and 3 species (Santa Fé, Floreana, and Fernandina) have been hunted into extinction. The giant tortoise population has plummeted from some 250,000 before humans arrived to just 20,000 now. Today, the main danger comes largely from introduced species, but there is a comprehensive rearing program to release tortoises back into the wild, most recently on Pinta Island.

Five of the remaining subspecies are found on the five main volcanoes of Isabela, and the other species are found on Santiago, Santa Cruz, San Cristóbal, Pinzón, and Española.

WHERE TO SEE THEM

Charles Darwin Research Station on Santa Cruz is the most famous place to see these

giant tortoise with saddle-shaped shell

BEST HIKES

view from Frigate Bird Hill

Bring your walking shoes, because rocky trails in the Galápagos are not best tackled in sandals. There are trails along pristine beaches, through forests of cacti, and along unworldly blackened lava trails, offering close encounters with wildlife and sweeping views over the archipelago.

Santa Fé (p. 62)

This small island midway between Santa Cruz and San Cristóbal offers trails through a forest of opuntia cacti, which grow up to 10 meters high, with Galápagos hawks circling overhead. Negotiate the rocky trail, and cross a steep ravine to view colonies of the yellowish Santa Fé iguana, endemic to the island.

Frigate Bird Hill, San Cristóbal (p. 65)

This is just one of many good hikes close to the main ports. Past the Interpretation Center are trails into the hills where frigate birds nest. The bay below has good snorkeling, or go to Playa Cabo de Horno, a quiet beach frequented by sea lions and backed by mangroves.

Sullivan Bay, Santiago (p. 71)

On the east side of the island, the trail along this blackened lava flow is a glimpse of what the earth must have looked like at the dawn of time. An eruption in 1897 left the area covered in mesmerizing patterns of *pahoehoe* lava. It's difficult to negotiate but a fascinating experience.

Bartolomé Island (p. 72)

This tiny island is the most photographed sight in the archipelago. A wooden staircase leads 114 meters up to a summit. In the foreground the mangroves are flanked on either side by twin half-moon beaches. Rising up behind is the famous Pinnacle Rock, a jagged lava formation. Descend to the short trail through mangroves between the two beaches, and cool off with some snorkeling with sea lions.

Sierra Negra, Isabela (p. 78)

By far the best trek is around this active volcano, the second-largest crater in the world. Take the short route to the fissure of lava cones at Volcano Chico, or hike longer into the yellow hills of the pungent Sulfur Mines.

amazing creatures. There is a breeding center with 11 subspecies and a walk-in enclosure. Lesser known but with a larger population is the Centro de Crianza breeding center on Isabela, which has more than 800 tortoises in eight separate enclosures. The best places to see tortoises in their natural environment are La Galapaguera, a reserve on San Cristóbal where tortoises reside in 12 hectares of dry forest, or the larger El Chato Tortoise Reserve, which fills the entire southwest corner of Santa Cruz.

Sea Turtles

There are four species of marine turtles in the archipelago. The eastern Pacific green turtle, also known as the black turtle (*tortuga negra*), is the most common species. Also present but rarely seen are the Pacific leatherback, Indo-Pacific hawksbill, and olive ridley turtles.

Green sea turtles are rarely seen in large numbers, preferring to swim alone, in couples, or next to their young. They usually weigh about 100 kg but can weigh up to 150 kg. The females are actually bigger than the males and can grow to 1.2 meters long. The mating season, November to January, is the best time to see them. Sea turtles must come ashore to lay eggs, and females often do this as many as eight times during the mating season.

WHERE TO SEE THEM

With a little luck, sea turtles can be seen swimming all over the archipelago, but the best-known nesting sites are Tortuga Bay on Santa Cruz, the beaches of Bartolomé, and Gardner Bay on Española.

Marine Iguanas

The only sea-faring lizards in the world, Galápagos marine iguanas are living proof of evolution. Scientists estimate that this species adapted over two or three million years from their land iguana cousins in order to find food underwater in the form of nutritious

Indo-Pacific hawksbill sea turtle

two marine iguanas resting on the shore

land iguana enjoying the shade

coastal seaweed. A flattened snout allows them to press themselves against the rocks to feed, a flattened tail propels them more effectively underwater, long claws grab the rocks firmly, and salt-eliminating glands in the nostrils cleanse the sea salt from their bodies. They can dive more than 12 meters below the surface.

Marine iguanas congregate in colonies for most of the year. During the mating season, which usually corresponds to the rainy season, males become more brightly colored, and their black coloring is punctuated by red, orange, and green spots.

WHERE TO SEE THEM

There are sizeable populations of marine iguanas on Seymour Norte, James Bay on Santiago, Gardner Bay and Punta Suárez on Española, and various sites on Isabela. However, the biggest population by far is at Punta Espinosa on Fernandina.

Land Iguanas

The Galápagos has seven subspecies of land iguana. They live in dry areas, and like their marine cousins, newborns are one of the few terrestrial creatures that have to fear the Galápagos hawk. They are also prey for many introduced species until they are big enough to defend themselves. As a result, the land iguana species on Santiago and Baltra are extinct, while those on other islands are endangered. A captive-breeding program at the Darwin Center is working to boost the population.

The Galápagos species are distinctively more yellow than greener mainland iguanas, particularly the subspecies on Santa Fé. There are also hybrids born from mating with marine iguanas. Like their marine cousins, the males can be very territorial, exhibiting brighter colors in the mating season and engaging in head-bashing battles with other males. They are famous for their head-nodding, a threat

BEST SNORKELING AND DIVING

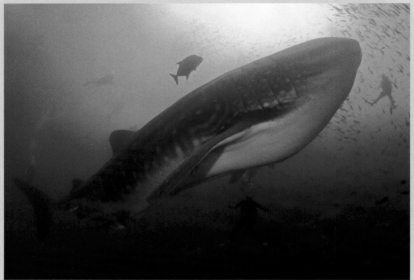

diving with a whale shark

The Galápagos may be the best destination worldwide for watching wildlife on land, but the marine marvels underwater are beyond belief. From snorkeling with playful sea lion pups and nonchalant sea turtles to diving with hammerheads and whale sharks, the Caribbean and Red Sea simply pale in comparison.

Gordon Rocks (p. 47)
One hour from Puerto Ayora, this site is for intermediate to advanced divers due to strong currents. Visibility is usually excellent, and you can watch schools of hammerheads, rays, moray eels, and marine turtles.

Kicker Rock (León Dormido), San Cristóbal (p. 69)
The narrow channel between the sheer walls of this volcanic tuff cone is a prime snorkeling spot. White-tipped reef sharks, sea turtles, and rays are commonly seen in the channel, while divers go deeper to see hammerheads. A visit is combined with snorkeling among a sea lion colony at nearby Isla Lobos.

Devil's Crown and Champion Island, Floreana (p. 84)
The jagged peaks of this submerged volcanic cone poke out of the water, hence its ominous name. Snorkel outside the ring or in the shallow inner chamber with tropical fish and occasional sharks. A visit is usually combined with snorkeling among a sea lion colony at Champion Island.

Gardner Bay, Española (p. 84)
On the northeast side of Española, this crescent beach offers snorkeling with a sea lion colony, stingrays, white-tipped sharks, and parrot fish. It's also an important nesting site for marine turtles.

Wolf and Darwin Islands (p. 86)
The ultimate diving experience, open only to live-aboard dive cruises, is found around these islands in the far north. Hundreds of hammerheads can be seen off Wolf, gigantic whale sharks cruise by June–November, and bottlenose dolphins are common at Darwin's Arch.

that can also be employed against humans if they get too close. Note that male iguanas can also whip their tails up if startled, so take care approaching them.

WHERE TO SEE THEM

The best places to see land iguanas are on Santa Cruz, Seymour Norte, Plaza Sur, and Santa Fé.

Galápagos Sea Lions

A close encounter with sea lions is for many people the highlight of a Galápagos trip. While other creatures show a mild disdain for humans, the sea lions are very communicative, and the pups are particularly playful in the water, which makes for an incredible snorkeling experience. After a hard day's fishing and playing, the sea lions sprawl over beaches and rocks, snoozing to replenish their oxygen supplies. Walking among a colony is another highlight of any trip. Outside their colonies, they are often found dozing on boats and docks.

The mature males can reach 2.5 meters in length, considerably bigger than the females. Males mate with about 10 to 15 females and can be very territorial, so be advised that, although most of this posturing is harmless, sea lions occasionally attack—it's the principal cause of animal injury to visitors in the Galápagos. Steer well clear of patrolling males, especially when snorkeling.

WHERE TO SEE THEM

The best places to snorkel with sea lions are at Enderby on Floreana's north shore, Isla Lobos on San Cristóbal, James Bay on Santiago, Gardner Bay on Española, Bartolomé, and Rábida. The best places to walk among a colony are on Plaza Sur and La Lobería on San Cristóbal as well as other beaches on the outskirts of Baquerizo Moreno.

Galápagos Fur Seal

Smaller than sea lions, with a thick furry coat, Galápagos fur seals are also harder to see

A sea lion rests on the rocky shores of the Galápagos Islands.

because they prefer shaded areas and cooler waters. We are lucky that these endearing animals with their bearlike snouts and small external ears exist at all after they were hunted to the brink of extinction in the 19th century. Although they are endemic to the islands, many seals have now emigrated to the coast of Peru. However, there are still estimated to be over 20,000 fur seals inhabiting the northern and western islands of Pinta, Marchena, Santiago, Isabela, and Fernandina.

WHERE TO SEE THEM

Fur seals are harder to see than sea lions, but the best opportunities are on Santiago, Isabela, Fernandina, and Genovesa.

Whales and Dolphins

There are many species of whales in the Galápagos, but it's rare to see them. The massive blue whale is an occasional visitor, but you're more likely to spot humpback whales breaching. The killer whales or orcas are the most feared, preying on sea lions and fur seals. They often swim in small groups and are known to use sonar to locate their prey. Far more commonly seen are schools of bottlenose dolphins surfing the bow waves of cruise boats and leaping in unison.

WHERE TO SEE THEM

The best spots to see humpback whales are west of Isabela and Fernandina from July to September. Whale sharks can only be seen on live-aboard dive cruises going to the northern islands of Wolf and Darwin. Dolphins can be spotted throughout the archipelago, usually in open seas from boats.

Boobies

The Spanish sailors who first discovered the Galápagos were very unimpressed by a bird that would simply peer at them curiously instead of fleeing, and so they called these birds *bobos* (stupid), and the name stuck. The insult to their intelligence is particularly

Dolphins can usually be seen in the open sea from cruise boats.

unfair because boobies are astonishingly adept at catching fish, dive-bombing the waters from as high as 25 meters before popping up to the surface and gulping down the luckless prey.

The blue-footed boobies are the most commonly seen because they nest on the ground. There are actually far more red-footed boobies in the archipelago, but these smaller birds tend to feed farther out to sea and are mainly found on more remote islands. They nest in trees and shrubs, in contrast to the other species. The masked boobies are the largest booby, with a wingspan of 1.5 meters. They nest on cliff edges, finding it difficult to take off from level ground. They are named for their black eye mask that contrasts with their bright white plumage.

A bird-watching highlight is a glimpse into a blue-footed booby's mating ritual: The male marches around, kicking his feet up high, then raises his beak skyward, whistles, and opens his wings.

WHERE TO SEE THEM

The blue-footed boobies are best seen on Seymour Norte, Punta Pitt on San Cristóbal, Española, and Genovesa. The largest colony of red-footed boobies is on Genovesa, but they can also be seen at Punta Pitt. The masked boobies can be seen on Genovesa, Española, and Punta Pitt, the latter being the only place where all three booby species can be seen together.

Frigate Birds

Frigate birds are most famous for the bright-red chest pouches that males inflate to the size of a basketball to attract females in the mating season. Once inflated, the male spends the entire day that way, calling and flapping his wings at passing females, hoping to attract one to the nest he has built for her. It's particularly romantic because once the female chooses the best-chested male, they mate for life. The sight of the inflated pouches is one of the highlights of bird-watching on the

masked booby

BEST WILDLIFE-WATCHING

A blue-footed booby displays part of his mating dance.

You won't be squinting through binoculars for glimpses of wildlife in the Galápagos – the animals display themselves proudly and fearlessly, and every excursion brings unforgettable sights.

Charles Darwin Research Station, Santa Cruz (p. 59)

No Galápagos trip is complete without visiting the giant tortoise enclosures and learning about the station's successful repopulation program.

Seymour Norte (p. 63)

Bird-watching heaven is found on this tiny island near Santa Cruz. Decide which has the most interesting mating ritual – boobies marching around showing off their bright blue feet or frigates inflating their red chests to the size of a basketball.

Plaza Sur (p. 63)

This tiny islet hosts the largest sea lion colony in the archipelago. Watch them lounging on the rocks and tending their pups, but keep your distance from the cranky bulls.

Punta Espinosa, Fernandina (p. 81)

Fernandina's only visitor site is home to the islands' largest marine iguana colony, along with a sea lion population and the biggest breeding site for flightless cormorants, birds who have swapped flying for diving to the ocean floor.

Punta Suárez, Española (p. 85)

On the west side of Española is the biggest breeding site in the world for waved albatross. Nicknamed "albatross airport," it's the best place to see these magnificent birds take off, land, and perform their dancing mating ritual.

archipelago. There are two species of frigates on the islands that are very similar in appearance, and both have the famous red sacs. They have a wide wingspan that can reach over two meters, but they are unable to swim.

WHERE TO SEE THEM

The best places to see frigates are Seymour Norte, Punta Pitt on San Cristóbal, Española, and Genovesa.

Waved Albatross

If you don't go to Española, you probably won't see the largest seabird in the archipelago. Nearly the entire world population of the waved albatross nests on this island from April to November before migrating to Peru. With a wingspan of 2.5 meters, they are one of the biggest birds on the islands, and it's quite a sight to see them taking off and landing. Española gets so busy in mating season that landing areas, most famously Punta Suárez, are nicknamed "albatross airports."

True to the Galápagos tradition, like boobies and frigates the albatross has an entertaining mating ritual. The couples perform an elaborate courtship display, clacking their bills together, sky calling, and dancing around in a synchronized circular walk. They sometimes do this for several hours, and the island turns into a kind of open-air avian disco.

WHERE TO SEE THEM

You can only see these birds on Española, especially Punta Suárez.

Galápagos Penguins

Galápagos penguins are the only penguins found in the northern hemisphere (the equator cuts across the north of Isabela) and at just 35 centimeters tall, they are one of the smallest penguins in the world. They evolved from the Humboldt penguins that inhabit the coast of Chile but have retained much of their original insulation. So while other species like iguanas and sea lions warm up on the rocks,

The dominant male frigate bird expresses his authority over his family.

the penguins struggle to cool down by swimming, standing with their wings out at 45-degree angles and even panting rapidly. They rise early and spend most of the day swimming and fishing before returning to their colonies in the afternoon. You're most likely to see them standing around on the rocks, but in the water they are quite a sight—streaking after fish at speeds up to 40 kilometers per hour.

WHERE TO SEE THEM

The largest colonies are on Fernandina and Isabela, with far smaller colonies on Floreana and Bartolomé.

Flightless Cormorants

Flightless cormorants are proof that evolution is not all about gaining skills but also about losing them. These birds spend so much time in water that, with no predators to fear on land, they have lost their ability to fly (the only species of cormorant to have done so).

They have neither the chest muscles nor the wingspan to take to the air, but instead have long necks, strong kicking legs, and webbed feet that make them experts at catching fish, eels, and even octopuses underwater.

They have an unusual courtship ritual, although you're unlikely to see it, as it takes place underwater. The pair performs an aquatic "dance," swimming back and forth past each other before the male leads the female to the surface to mate.

WHERE TO SEE THEM

You can only see these birds on Fernandina and western Isabela.

Endemic Gulls

There are over 35,000 swallow-tailed gulls nesting throughout the archipelago. These attractive birds sport a black head, a distinctive red eye ring, white and gray body, and red feet. The lava gull is thought to be the rarest gull in the world, with only 400 mating pairs

waved albatross nesting on Española Island

Galápagos penguin

nesting exclusively in the Galápagos. Their dark gray plumage makes them difficult to pick out from the lava rocks they inhabit.

WHERE TO SEE THEM

Endemic gulls are usually seen flying over the ocean or nesting on rocky shores and cliffs. There are large nesting sites at Española and Genovesa.

Greater Flamingos

Their distinctive pink color makes these birds an attractive sight in the lagoons around the archipelago. They feed on shrimp by filtering through the salty lagoon water, and this shellfish diet turns them pink from their original white.

WHERE TO SEE THEM

The best places to see flamingos are Punta Cormorant on Floreana, Red Beach on Rábida, Puerto Villamil on Isabela, and Cerro Dragon and Bachas Beach on Santa Cruz.

The Galápagos Hawk

Out of the water, this fearless bird is the largest natural predator on the islands. It eats everything from baby iguanas and lizards to small birds, rodents, and insects as well as scavenging on dead animals. It also has a highly unusual mating system known as co-operative polyandry: Up to four males mate with a single female, then help to incubate and raise the young.

WHERE TO SEE THEM

The hawks are found throughout the archipelago but good spots include the Santa Cruz highlands, Santa Fé, James Bay on Santiago, Bartolomé, Rábida, and Punta Suárez on Española.

Darwin's Finches

These tiny birds are arguably the most important species in the Galápagos from a scientific viewpoint. The 13 species of finches with varied beak shapes were the most

swallow-tailed gull

important inspiration for Charles Darwin's evolution theory. The key to the finches' survival, as Darwin noted, is the beak. Short, thick beaks enable ground finches to crack hard seeds, while longer, slimmer bills allow other species to probe crevices for insects and eat cacti or flowers. Finches are remarkably resourceful birds and are one of the few species to use tools to find prey. Woodpecker and mangrove finches use a cactus spine or small twig to get at grubs burrowed deep in tree branches.

The sharp-billed ground finch is the most unusual species, and a little sinister. It is nicknamed the "vampire finch" for its habit of pecking at the base of a booby's tail until it can drink a trickle of blood. This species also rolls other birds' eggs until they break and then eats the insides.

WHERE TO SEE THEM

The different species are found throughout the archipelago, but the best places to see them are in the San Cristóbal highlands, James Bay on Santiago, Punta Suárez on Española, and Darwin Bay Beach on Genovesa.

Sharks

The most common sharks in the Galápagos are the docile white-tipped sharks and black-tipped sharks, which eat plankton and small fish. They tend to rest under rocks and in caves but are also commonly seen swimming close to shore.

For the more adventurous, watch for scary-looking hammerhead sharks. Large schools of 30 or 40 of these incredible creatures are commonly encountered when diving, although they can occasionally be seen while snorkeling at Kicker Rock (León Dormido) or off the north shore of Floreana.

The largest shark in the archipelago is the huge whale shark, up to 20 meters long, found only on the outlying islands of Darwin and Wolf, visited mainly by dedicated dive boats.

Galápagos hawk

a mangrove finch, Tortuga Bay

stingray

WHERE TO SEE THEM

Reef sharks are found all over the archipelago, but you are most likely to encounter them while snorkeling in the waters around Española, Floreana, Seymour Norte, Bartolomé, Las Tintoreras on Isabela, and Kicker Rock (León Dormido) on San Cristóbal. The larger Galápagos shark is another species that can be seen in these areas.

Divers can see hammerhead sharks at Kicker Rock and off Floreana, and whale sharks on Darwin and Wolf.

Rays

The most common rays you will see while snorkeling or diving are stingrays, whose wings can span up to two meters, but be careful of the sting that can whip up if you startle them. They are also found resting on sandy beaches, so watch where you step. Most

spectacular are the brightly colored golden rays, the massive, six-meter-long manta rays, and the rarer spotted eagle rays, found mainly in deeper waters.

WHERE TO SEE THEM

Rays are seen all over the archipelago and are easiest to see when snorkeling or diving, although they are also visible from boats. Good snorkel sites include Kicker Rock (León Dormido), Gardner Bay, and Bartolomé, and good dive sites include Gordon Rocks, Santa Fé, Mosquera, Daphne Minor, and Cousins Rock.

Fish

Choosing highlights from the vast array of fish in the waters around the archipelago is tricky, but on the top of the must-see list are the multicolored parrot fish; clown fish;

a sally lightfoot crab

moorish idol, with its long dorsal fin over a body banded with black, yellow, and white; and the orange, black, and white harlequin wrasse, a hermaphrodite that can spontaneously change sex from female to male.

WHERE TO SEE THEM

You should be able to see many of these fish on snorkeling excursions throughout the archipelago.

Crustaceans

Nobody expects crabs to be a highlight of a Galápagos trip, but you'll be surprised at how eye-catching some of the invertebrates are. Of the 100 crab species in the islands, the most colorful is the bright-red sally lightfoot crab, named for its fast movement across water over short distances. They are easily startled and can give a nasty pinch. They need to be fast to avoid the attention of herons and moray eels.

WHERE TO SEE THEM

Crabs can be seen on rocky shores and beaches throughout the archipelago. Prime locations for the sally lightfoot crabs include Bachas Beach, Seymour Norte, James Bay, and Gardner Bay.

VISITING THE ISLANDS

There are basically two ways to see the Galápagos: on a cruise or on a land-based tour. Cruises have historically been the most popular, and advantages include the opportunity to travel farther, cover more sites, and spend more time there without needing to get back to port at dusk. There are also many sites only accessible to cruise tours, and there is less environmental impact than staying on land, with none of the associated pollution from hotels. The drawbacks are that you are on a boat with the same group for several days with a fixed schedule, which doesn't suit everyone. Seasickness is also a factor, even on the best boats. With the wide choice of classes available, it's important to remember that, by and large, you get what you pay for. You could save a few hundred dollars by opting for the cheapest boat, but you'll end up with a guide with less knowledge, less comfort, and probably worse seasickness.

Land-based tours are becoming increasingly popular, particularly for those not suited to spending a long time on a boat. Many operators organize short tours based on one island, or you can do an island-hopping tour. However, with the wide availability of day tours in Puerto Ayora and regular ferries between the three main populated islands (San Cristóbal, Santa Cruz, and Isabela), increasing numbers of budget travelers are shunning tours and doing it themselves, saving a lot of money. Bear in mind, though, that doing it this way restricts

you to day tours close to the main islands, and islands such as Genovesa, Española, Santiago, and Fernandina as well as the better sites on Floreana and Santa Fé become off-limits.

Whatever you decide to do, it's important that you don't get preoccupied with a checklist. Eight days (or even five days) in the Galápagos is an incredible experience to be savored, so don't ruin your enjoyment of it by becoming obsessed with seeing it all.

Cruise Tours

Most cruises are five to eight days. There are also four-day itineraries, but when you consider that half a day at the beginning and end is spent traveling, a minimum of five days is recommended, and eight days is preferable if you can afford it. In five days, the most common cruise itineraries start at Santa Cruz, taking in Puerto Ayora, the highlands, Seymour Norte, and the South Plazas, then head either north or south. Northern tours usually include Bartolomé, Santiago, and Genovesa, while southern itineraries usually take in Santa Fé, San Cristóbal, Floreana, and Española. There is also a slightly less frequent and more expensive western itinerary that includes Isabela and Fernandina. Eight-day tours usually combine two of these three routes (north and west, north and south, or west and south). It's not possible to see all of the above islands in eight days, and while cruises for longer than eight days do exist, they are rare and mostly dedicated dive trips. Dive tours are the only ones that reach the most remote islands of Darwin, Wolf, and Marchena. Note that new rules introduced for 2012, which aim to protect the most popular visitor sites, prohibit boats from visiting the same site in a 14-day period (previously the limit was seven days). This has forced cruise operators to change their itineraries.

There are five classes of tour boats—economy, tourist, tourist superior, first, and luxury—and trips range from four to eight days, with occasional special charters of 11 and 15 days. Whatever length of tour you opt for, there's no escaping that it's not cheap. Prices range from less than $750 per person for a five-day economy-class trip to $5,000 for eight days on a luxury-class vessel. Note that arrival and departure days are counted as tour days. Prices include food, accommodations, transfers to and from your boat, trained guides, and all your shore visits. The airfare and insurance are paid separately, and you'll need to factor in tips for the crew, plus alcoholic and soft drinks on board. Note that single cabin supplements are usually very high. It doesn't hurt to ask, but you're far better off sharing a cabin.

Itineraries are strictly controlled by the National Park Service to regulate the impact of visitors on delicate sites. Every cruise has a tight schedule, and the feeling of being herded around doesn't suit everyone, but console yourself that cruises have far less impact on the environment than land-based tours; plus you get to see far more.

CRUISE BOATS
Economy Boats
Prices for boats in the economic class range $1,000-1,250 per person per week, but there are frequent last-minute deals because older visitors booking from abroad tend to avoid the most basic boats. You may be lucky and have a good experience, but note that every aspect of the service on these small boats, which carry 8-16 passengers, will be basic: Class One guides have a low level of training and knowledge and often a poor level of English; cabins are tiny and more prone to rocking, so seasickness is worse; and the food will likely be uninspiring.

© CARLOS GONZALEZ

the *Monserrat*, a first-class yacht

The baths are shared. Economy boats also have smaller engines and can't cover distances as great as the bigger boats can.

While this level of boat suits some budget travelers, they are losing popularity to land-based tours, and there are very few of these boats at the islands now (the *Sulidae* is one example). You should also consider that the Galápagos is probably a once-in-a-lifetime experience, so paying a bit more for better service is advisable.

Moderately Priced Boats

Tourist-class and tourist superior-class boats are the most common cruise choice in the islands. These medium-size sailboats or motorboats hold 10-16 passengers. Everything is better quality than the economy boats—better cabins (though still small), more varied food, and Class Two guides with a higher level of knowledge and better English. These boats also have bigger engines so are faster and often cover longer distances, including remote islands such as Genovesa. While the service is not as good as first-class boats, overall these boats offer the best deal and attract a mixed range of clients—from backpackers to locals and older foreign travelers.

Boats in these categories include *Aida Maria, Amigo, Angelito, Angelique, Daphne, Darwin, Encantada, Floreana, Galápagos Vision I* and *Vision II, Golondrina, Guantanamera, Intrepido, Merack, New Flamingo, Rumba, Samba, Spondylus,* and *Yolita*. Costs range $1,200-1,600 per person per week for tourist class and $1,600-2,000 per person per week for tourist superior class.

First-Class Boats

This is probably the best cruise experience you can get on the islands—these boats are far more comfortable but still have a small capacity (mainly 16-26 passengers) to retain an intimate group atmosphere. They can also cover longer distances, and most include visits to the fascinating western islands of Isabela and Fernandina. Cabins are more comfortable, with beds rather than bunks, and the decor makes the interior a pleasant place to spend time, unlike many cheaper boats, where you want to escape the interior any chance you get. The interior is usually air-conditioned. These are also much sturdier yachts, so seasickness is less of a problem. Guides have to be Class Three, so they must hold a degree in natural sciences, usually biology or geology, and speak nearly fluent English.

Boats include the *Archipel II, Cachalote, Cormorant II, Diamante, Eden, Eric, Letty, Estrella del Mar, Fragata, Galaxy, Mary Anne, Millennium, Monserrat, Nemo I* and *II, Queen Beatriz, Queen of Galápagos, Sagitta, San Jose, Santa Cruz, Tip Top II, III,* and *IV, The Beagle,* and *The Voyager.* Prices here range $2,000-3,800 per person for a week.

Deluxe Tours

While the largest cruise ships are thankfully a thing of the past in the Galápagos, there is still demand, mainly from older travelers, for a deluxe tour with standards comparable to good hotels on the mainland. Most of the these ships have capacity for more than 40 passengers, and the biggest, such as *Galápagos Explorer II, Galápagos Legend,* and *Xpedition,* cater to 100. The food is gourmet, the guides are the best in the archipelago, and there are many facilities on board to keep you busy at the end of the day's tours: spas, massages, gyms, jetted tubs, swimming pools, even karaoke bars, although some would pay money to avoid the latter. Tours and meals are announced by loudspeaker, and guides are Class Three. Note, however, that you should not book these tours expecting a comparable level of luxury as found in top-class hotels on land—cabin sizes still do not compare to five-star hotels.

The biggest benefit of these larger boats is,

like the first-class yachts, that they are faster and so can reach the outlying islands. Best of all, rolling with the sea is minimized, so you're far less likely to get seasick, although it's still possible. The biggest drawback is the feeling of being herded around in a large group. It's more difficult to have an intimate experience of the wildlife when dozens of other passengers are chatting and clicking their cameras. Due to the size of the group, there is very little flexibility in the tours, and schedules are set in stone.

Cruise ships include *Alta, Anahi, Athala, Beluga, Coral I* and *II, Flamingo, Endeavor, Explorer II, Isabela II, Lammer Law, La Pinta, Legend, Odyssey, Parranda,* and *Xpedition.* Luxury-class tours start at $3,800 per person per week and climb to over $5,000 per person.

Guides

While the boat you travel on is very important, a good or bad guide can make or break your trip. There's no escaping the fact that, in most cases, you get what you pay for. The good news is that all Galápagos guides are trained and licensed by the National Park Service, and they have all received further training in recent years as part of the Ecuadorian government's action to confront the islands' environmental problems. Guides are qualified in one of three classes, in ascending order of quality: Class One, usually on economy boats or handling land-based tours, have the lowest level of knowledge and English; Class Two, on tourist and tourist superior class boats, are more knowledgeable and often very good; and Class Three guides, on first-class and luxury boats, are the real experts and have all studied natural sciences at university. All guides should speak at least two languages, but Class One guides often speak little besides Spanish. Every guide has to pass rigorous examinations every three years and complete a training course on the islands every six years to keep his or her certification. When booking a tour, ask about your guide's

VISITING THE ISLANDS

© RAMIRO SALAZAR

Deluxe cruise ships like *La Pinta* are able to reach outlying sites faster than other cruise ships.

specific qualifications and what language he or she speaks.

LIFE ON BOARD
Daily Routine

When you arrive on your boat, unless you're in first-class or deluxe, your first reaction may be: "I didn't think the cabin would be *that* small." But bear in mind that your room is really just for sleeping—you'll have far too much to look at outside on deck and at the visitor sites.

You'll meet the rest of the tour group, and your guide will introduce him or herself and the rest of the crew before going through the tour schedule. Guides will also explain the park rules, which you must follow.

Most days have an early start (breakfast at 7 A.M. or earlier) to give you the maximum time at the island sites (and also to get there before the day tours). Most boats tend to travel overnight to save time, and it's one of the joys

of the cruise to wake up in a new place. The morning visits usually take 2-3 hours, including the *panga* ride to shore. Your guide will direct the group along the path or down the beach, explaining what you're seeing and filling in relevant natural-history details as you go. Be understanding if your guide seems overly concerned about keeping the group together and making everyone stick to the trail; remember that some visitors unwittingly cause damage, and the tour group is the guide's responsibility. Just because you've paid a lot of money doesn't mean you can do whatever you want. The same sentiment applies when your guides insist that you wear a lifejacket during *panga* rides; they face fines and jail time if they're caught with passengers not wearing them.

Back on board, you'll find your cabin clean and lunch ready. The midday meal is casual—a buffet on cruise ships and fixed menus on smaller vessels. You may find yourself

TRAVELS WITH CHARLIE

As I was walking along I met two large tortoises, each of which must have weighed at least two hundred pounds: one was eating a piece of cactus, and as I approached, it stared at me and slowly walked away; the other gave a deep hiss, and drew in its head. These huge reptiles, surrounded by the black lava, the leafless shrubs, and large cacti, seemed to my fancy like some antediluvian animals.

Charles Darwin in *The Voyage of the Beagle,* on his first encounter with giant tortoises

surprisingly hungry after all that hiking and snorkeling, but don't overeat, as you may get lethargic and more prone to seasickness if the boat is traveling after lunch. Lots of water and fruit is important to keep your energy and hydration levels up. Your guide will announce the departure time for the afternoon excursion; there's usually an hour's break.

Afternoon visits are similar to the morning, although it's considerably hotter, so take a hat and plenty of sunblock. Late afternoon is famously the best time for photography. Don't miss the incomparable opportunities to snorkel, for many people the highlight of their trip. Where else in the world can you swim with sea lions, turtles, stingrays, and sharks? Wetsuits are handy, especially in the cold season, but not necessary in the warm season; wearing just a swimsuit, most people can last about half an hour in the water before getting chilled.

There's usually some time before dinner to freshen up and enjoy a drink while watching the sunset (just after 6 P.M. year-round). Dinner is the most important meal of the day, and this is your chance to fill up. Formality and the quality of the food depend on the class of cruise. After dinner, your guide will review what you saw today and preview tomorrow's schedule.

The higher-class vessels often have after-dinner entertainment; otherwise it's a case of swapping tales with your fellow passengers. Alcohol is available, but try not to overdo it—you don't want the next morning's tour ruined by a hangover and interrupted sleep. Bear in mind that drinks are comparatively pricey and not included in the tour. You may be surprised to be nodding off by 9 P.M. Get plenty of rest because, after all, you didn't come to the Galápagos for the nightlife.

Tipping

It's customary to tip at the end of the cruise. Remember that, although your tour is expensive, in a country as unequal as Ecuador, the big bucks don't filter down to the lowest level; the crew as well as the guide will very much appreciate your tip. Obviously use your own judgment on how much to give, and your tip should reflect the level of service. Between 5 and 10 percent of the price of the cruise is considered normal. Tip the guide separately, and use the tip box for the rest of the crew.

BOOKING AND PAYMENT

Booking a tour to the Galápagos can be done anywhere—from thousands of kilometers away at home in your own country to an agency in Puerto Ayora the night before the cruise leaves. In general, the farther away you are from the islands, the more it costs. You can save up to 50 percent of the total price by booking your tour last-minute in Ecuador. Even greater savings can be made booking last-minute in the Galápagos. However, bear in mind that it's very much a question of luck to get what you want, particularly if you have a specific itinerary in mind.

To book a cruise from abroad, a deposit of at least $200 per person (via wire transfer or Western Union) is required. Ecuador does not permit the use of credit cards for any payments by Internet or telephone, so they can't be used without the owner, the card, and the passport being present in Ecuador. This is to combat credit card fraud. Even so, only a handful of boats accept credit cards for payment in person, and these still require partial payment in cash or traveler's checks. However, you can pay for your flights with credit cards.

Many travel agencies in Quito and Guayaquil advertise tours, so shopping around is a good idea. The more time you browse, the more likely you are to find a good deal, so it pays to be patient. The best deals come when agencies are desperate to fill the last few spaces on a tour, and you can save between 25 and 50 percent. Note that the best last-minute deals are on the better classes of boats. Deposits range 10-50 percent, depending on the boat

and tour operator. You are normally required to have paid in full 30 days before departure, unless it's a last-minute deal.

The biggest savings can be made by flying to Puerto Ayora, checking into a cheap hotel, and browsing the agencies on the waterfront for last-minute deals. Securing more than 50 percent of the original price is possible, but it's all a question of luck and far less likely in high season (Dec.-Apr. and July-Aug.). If you are doing it this way, consider avoiding the shorter cruises that frequent sites on or close to Santa Cruz because many of these you can do yourself on day trips.

Ensure you get an itinerary and all the details of what you are paying for printed out. Some travelers find that they pay for what they thought was a superior boat only to get landed with an economy vessel, so it's worthwhile getting the name of the boat and researching it online. Direct all complaints concerning tours, before or after, to the port captain (*capitanía del puerto*) if you booked in the islands, and to the agency directly if you booked in Quito or outside the country.

Land Tours and Independent Travel

Sleeping and eating on a boat is not for everybody, and if you are particularly prone to seasickness, consider a land-based itinerary. These are becoming increasingly common, both on organized tours and for independent travelers. Most commonly you will be based in Santa Cruz, but itineraries that take in San Cristóbal and/or Isabela are also popular. Five-day tours start at about $600 per person, but savings can be had last-minute.

However, note that many land-based itineraries take in sights close to the main ports, which can easily be visited independently. If you want to do it yourself, you can usually

find accommodations in the ports for as little as $20 per person per night, and many of the surrounding beaches are free to visit. As well as seeing sites on Santa Cruz, San Cristóbal, and Isabela, day tours run regularly from Santa Cruz to Bartolomé, Seymour Norte, the Plaza Islands, Floreana, and Santa Fé. The other islands are out of bounds to day tours. Doing it this way, you could easily spend just $500 in five days, not including flights. Note that there may be no escaping seasickness even on land-based tours because you will spend plenty of time on boats shuttling to and from the port, and they are smaller boats that roll around more.

WHERE TO STAY

There are plenty of accommodations in the three main ports. Puerto Ayora on Santa Cruz has the widest range, with double rooms from just $30 per night up to $400. Baquerizo Moreno on San Cristóbal has a good range and is quieter, and Puerto Villamil on Isabela also has a small range of accommodations, although the island's tourism offering is expanding. On Floreana, there are just two hotels. The best hotels on the islands are often booked up in high season (Christmas-Easter), but cheap accommodations are usually available in all the ports. Note that rates at the top-end hotels are very high, so you are usually better off booking an all-inclusive tour if you want to stay at this level of accommodations.

DAY TRIPS

For land-based tours, there are plenty of day trips running out of Puerto Ayora on Santa Cruz. If you book a land-based tour, many of these are included, but some can easily be visited independently or booked last-minute a day or so before.

Tortuga Bay and Charles Darwin Station can easily be visited independently on foot. The cheapest tours are the bay tour ($35 pp), which takes in La Lobería, where you can snorkel with sea lions; Playa de los Perros, where marine iguanas and various birds are seen; Las Tintoreras; channels where sharks are often found; and the lava rock fissures of Las Grietas, easily visited independently. The highlands tour goes to El Chato Tortoise Reserve, the nearby lava tunnels, and the collapsed craters Los Gemelos. Alternatively, see these highland sights independently with a taxi driver for about $30 for a half-day.

For visits to nearby islands, the cheaper tours go to Floreana ($75 pp) and Santa Fé ($60 pp). However, bear in mind that many of the best sites are closed to day tours and only accessible to cruises. Indeed, the Santa Fé day tour cannot

Herons frequent hotel pool patios.

even land on the island but is restricted to snorkeling offshore. A tour to Isabela costs $80 per person and tours to Plaza Sur, Seymour Norte, and Bartolomé cost considerably more—about $125 per person—and may rise further. These are deliberate price hikes imposed by the national park to restrict visitor numbers at the busiest sites.

If you're based on other islands, options are more restricted. In Baquerizo Moreno on San Cristóbal, there is an Interpretation Center on the edge of town as well as several beaches with wildlife, including La Lobería, which has a large sea lion colony. For tours, the boat trip to Isla Lobos and Kicker Rock (León Dormido) for $60 per person is one of the best day trips available on the archipelago, including snorkeling with sharks and sea lions. In the highlands, you can hire a taxi for $10 per hour and visit the freshwater lake of Laguna El Junco, the giant tortoise reserve La Galapaguera, and Puerto Chino, an isolated beach.

In Puerto Villamil on Isabela, there are snorkeling excursions at Las Tintoreras on the edge of town, and a tortoise breeding center within walking distance. The best excursion is a hike to Sierra Negra, the second-largest volcanic crater in the world. There is a half-day and full-day guided hike ($40 pp).

Tour Operators and Last-Minute Deals

Following is a list of reputable tour operators. In general, prices get cheaper the closer you are to the Galápagos. Booking from the United States costs $2,000-5,000 per person, and prices in the United Kingdom can be even higher. U.S. and UK prices all include flights to Ecuador and the islands. The advantage of booking with an operator based in the United States or the United Kingdom is that everything is organized in advance, and you are guaranteed your chosen itinerary. Prices in Quito and Guayaquil tend to range $1,000-3,000 per person, including flights to the islands but not including flights to Ecuador, and frequent last-minute discounts are available. In Puerto Ayora in the Galápagos, prices are frequently 25 percent cheaper than in Quito and Guayaquil. Booking locally can get you a great deal, but it requires flexibility, and quality is more variable.

IN THE UNITED STATES

Adventure Associates (13150 Coit Rd., Suite 110, Dallas, TX 75240, U.S. tel. 800/527-2500, U.S. fax 972/783-1286, www.adventure-associates.com) organizes cruises and land-based tours with Ecuadorian-based operator Metropolitan Touring from just $1,100 per person, not including flights.

Avalon Cruising (5301 S Federal Circle, Littleton, CO 80123, U.S. tel. 303/703-7000, www.avalonwaterways.com) has a 10-day Ecuador and Galápagos tour, including a four-night cruise, from $3,898 per person.

Gate1travel (455 Maryland Dr., Fort Washington, PA 19034, U.S. tel. 215/572-7676 or 800/682-3333) has a range of Galápagos tours combined with tours of Ecuador and Peru. A seven-day tour with three nights in the Galápagos costs from $1,999 per person.

Holbrook Travel (3540 NW 13th St., Gainesville, FL 32609, U.S. tel. 800/451-7111, www.holbrooktravel.com) has a 10-day tour that includes a seven-night cruise on the MV *Floreana* for $3,025 per person.

Mountain Travel-Sobek (1266 66th St., Emeryville, CA 94608, U.S. tel. 510/594-6000 or 888/831-7526, www.mtsobek.com) has a nine-day land-based tour to the Galápagos for $3,295 per person as well as nine-day cruises from $3,795 per person.

Nature Expeditions International (7860 Peters Rd., Suite F-103, Plantation, FL 33324, U.S. tel. 954/693-8852 or 800/869-0639, U.S. fax 954/693-8854, www.naturexp.com) offers educational adventure travel for older active travelers, including a 12-day Ecuador and Galápagos tour from $4,235 per person.

Wilderness Travel (1102 9th St., Berkeley, CA 94710, U.S. tel. 800/368-2794, U.S. fax 510/558-2489, www.wildernesstravel.com) has nine-day tours from $4,595 per person.

Wildland Adventures (3516 NE 155th St., Seattle, WA 98155, U.S. tel. 206/365-0686 or 800/345-4453, U.S. fax 206/363-6615, www.wildland.com), an award-winning ecotourism company, has eight-day tours that include a five-day cruise from $2,795 per person.

IN THE UNITED KINGDOM

Andean Trails (33 Sandport St., Edinburgh EH6 6EQ, UK tel. 131/467-7086, www.andeantrails.co.uk) offers land-based tours and cruises. A 10-day land-based tour starts at $2,000 per person, and an eight-day cruise on a tourist-superior yacht is $1,800 per person.

Audley Travel (New Mill, New Mill Lane, Witney OX29 9SX, UK tel. 1993/838-635, www.audleytravel.com) offers cruises and land-based packages in the Galápagos using tourist-superior and first-class boats from $3,160 per person for seven days.

CTS Horizons (Golden Cross House, 8 Duncannon St., London WC2N 4JF, UK tel. 20/7868-5590, www.ctshorizons.com) offers a 12-day tour of Ecuador including a seven-night Galápagos cruise from $3,395 per person.

Families Worldwide (UK tel. 845/051-4567, www.familiesworldwide.co.uk) is a specialist family adventure company offering tailor-made trips to Ecuador and the Galápagos. A 10-day land and sea tour that includes a three-night cruise and two nights in the Finch Bay Eco Hotel costs $4,710 per person adults, $3,450 per person children.

Journey Latin America (12-13 Healthfield Terrace, Chiswick, London W4 4JE, UK tel. 20/8747-8315, www.journeylatinamerica.co.uk) specializes in Latin America and has five-day Galápagos cruises on first-class yachts from $2,440 per person, eight-day cruises from $4,720 per person.

Last Frontiers (The Mill, Quainton Rd., Waddesdon, Buckinghamshire HP18 0LP, UK tel. 1296/653-000, www.lastfrontiers.com) offers tailor-made holidays that include cruises on a choice of over 20 vessels as well as land-based tours staying at the Finch Bay Hotel and the Albemarle Hotel. Cruise prices range $2,850-5,150 per person for seven nights. Full Ecuador and Galápagos packages, including flights, cost from $3,500 per person.

Llama Travel (Oxford House, 49A Oxford Rd., London N4 3EY, UK tel. 20/7263-3000, www.llamatravel.com) offers a 14-day tour of

Ecuador and the Galápagos that includes five days in Ecuador and an eight-day cruise on a first-class, 16-berth yacht from $4,660 per person.

Pura Aventura (18 Bond St., Brighton BN1 1RD, UK tel. 1273/676-712, www.pura-aventura.com) offers 4-15-day cruises on tourist-, first-, and luxury-class vessels such as the *Samba, Beagle, Sagitta,* and *Eclipse.* Private land-based trips are also offered, staying in hotels such as Casa Iguana on San Cristóbal and the Albemarle Hotel on Isabela. Eight-day Galápagos cruises cost from $2,000 per person.

Select Latin America (Canterbury Court, 1-3 Brixton Rd., London SW9 6DE, UK tel. 20/7407-1478, www.selectlatinamerica.co.uk) has been running specialist escorted Galápagos tours since 1985 and has a huge range of bespoke cruise options, including sailing yachts (*Beagle, Sagitta, and Mary Anne*) and larger luxury cruise ships (*Eclipse, La Pinta, Isabela II*). There are also small group charters on the *Reina Silvia* with expert tour leaders. Prices range from about $1,260 for a four-day cruise on the *Coral* to over $4,740 for eight days on the *Eclipse.* Land-based tours can be arranged at the Finch Bay Hotel on Santa Cruz or the Albemarle Hotel on Isabela.

Sunvil Traveller (UK tel. 20/8758-4774, www.sunvil.co.uk) offers tailor-made trips, including a selection of quality 3-14-night cruises on small sailing ships and larger motor yachts as well as land-based trips on Santa Cruz and Isabela. There is also a specialist walking tour of Isabela. Three-night cruises cost from $2,360 per person, including flights from Quito.

Voyages Jules Verne (UK tel. 845/166-7035; www.vjv.com) has a 16-night "Treasures of Ecuador" tour (from $6,790 per person) that includes a six-night Galápagos cruise on the MS *Galápagos Explorer II* with an on-board Charles Darwin lecture.

Wildlife Worldwide (UK tel. 845/130-6982, www.wildlifeworldwide.com) offers a 12-day land-based island-hopping itinerary (from $4,720 pp) that takes in five islands.

IN ECUADOR

All Ecuadorian tour operators do last-minute deals. You can easily save 25 percent off the original local price at tour operators in Quito, even greater savings compared with prices quoted in the United States.

Quito

Quito has more tour companies than ever, and many of them are excellent. This is the best place to pick up good deals on trips to the Galápagos, and there are regular last-minute discounts. Taking a guided tour also takes the worry out of traveling: Accommodations, food, and logistics are all sorted out for you. Bear in mind that not all operators in Quito have good reputations: Some overcharge and are under-qualified. The following operators are recommended for their quality, professionalism, and value. Most prices quoted here are the regular rates, not last-minute prices. Prices do not include flights to the islands (add about $400 per person for round-trip flights from Quito or Guayaquil).

Angermeyer Cruises (P.O. Box 17210088, Mariana de Jesús E7-113 at Pradera, tel. 2/323-7330, www.angermeyercruises.com) offers cruises on first-class sailboats, including the *Mary Anne, Sagitta,* and *Mandalay,* and the schooner MS *Beagle.* Five days on the *Sagitta* costs from $2,338 per person; eight days on the *Beagle* costs from $3,320 per person.

Enchanted Expeditions (De Las Alondras N45-102 at Los Lirios, tel. 2/334-0525, fax 2/334-0123, www.enchantedexpeditions. com) has cruises on the first-class rigged sailor *Cachalote* and the first-class motor yacht *Beluga.* Land extensions are offered at a choice of seven hotels and guesthouses on Santa Cruz and Isabela. Eight-day cruises cost from $2,300 per person.

Galápagos Tours (Amazonas 2331 at Veintimilla, tel. 2/254-6028, www.galapagostours.net) offers a wide range of cruises and land-based tours. A five-day cruise on the tourist superior-class *Aida Maria* costs from $1,380 per person, and eight days on the first-class *Eden* is $2,160 per person.

Galasam (Amazonas 1354 at Cordero, tel. 2/250-7079, www.galasam.com.ec) offers tours on the deluxe-class *Queen of Galápagos,* the first-class *Estrella de Mar,* and the tourist-class boat *Amigo* as well as diving cruises on the *Humboldt Explorer.* A four-day first-class cruise costs from $1,500 per person, eight days from $2,900 per person.

Guide2Galapagos (www.guide2galapagos. com) is run by **Sangay Touring** (Amazonas 1188 at Cordero, tel. 2/255-0180, www.sangay.com) and offers a wide range of last-minute deals on 50 different vessels in all classes, including four days in tourist class from $600 per person, eight days in luxury class from $2,600 per person.

Kem Pery Tours (Pinto 539 at Amazonas, tel. 2/222-6583, www.kempery.com) offers a wide range of cruises in all classes. Three-night cruises cost from $1,071 per person.

Metropolitan Touring (De los Palmeras N45-74 at Las Orquideas, tel. 2/298-8200, www.metropolitan-touring.com) is the largest tour operator in the country and was the first to organize high-quality Galápagos trips in the 1960s. It offers cruises on the MV *Santa Cruz, Isabela II,* and *La Pinta* as well as land-based tours from the Finch Bay Hotel. Four-day cruises cost from $1,500 per person, and eight-day cruises cost up to $4,935 per person. Information and bookings are available in the United States through **Adventure Associates** (13150 Coit Rd., Suite 110, Dallas, TX 75240, U.S. tel. 800/527-2500, U.S. fax 972/783-1286, www.adventure-associates.com).

Ninfa Tour (Amazonas N24-66 at Joaquin

Pinto, tel. 2/222-3124, www.galapagosninfatour.com) offers cheap land-based tours staying at Hotel Ninfa in Puerto Ayora and taking day trips as well as island-hopping itineraries. Five-day tours cost from $400 per person.

Nuevo Mundo Travel and Tours (18 de Septiembre E4-161 at Juan León Mera, tel. 2/250-9431, www.nuevomundotravel.com) was started in 1979 by a founder and former president of the Ecuadorian Ecotourism Association. Its tours and facilities, therefore, are among the most environmentally conscious in Ecuador. Land-based tours cost from $500 per person for four days in economy hotels, from $900 per person for four days in deluxe hotels. Cruises start at $1,600 per person for six days in tourist superior-class and from $2,295 per person in deluxe class.

Safari Tours (Reina Victoria N25-33 at Colon, tel. 2/255-2505 or 2/222-0426, fax 2/222-0426 or 2/222-3381, www.safari.com.ec) is one of the most frequently recommended operators in the country. Safari has a complete Galápagos database and can book last-minute spaces or make reservations online. Browse their deals of the week on the website. Last-minute deals are available from $1,600 per person for eight-day cruises.

Scuba Iguana (Amazonas 1004 at Wilson, tel. 2/290-6666, www.scubaiguana.com) is one of the leading diving specialists in Ecuador and organizes both live-aboard dive cruises and land-based tours with diving day trips. Daily dive prices cost $200 per person. Live-aboard dive cruises range $3,800-4,700 per person for a week.

Surtrek (Amazonas N23-87 at Wilson, tel. 2/223-1534, fax 2/250-0540, www.surtrek.org) offers a wide range of Galápagos tours and last-minute deals in all cruise classes as well as land-based tours and specialist diving tours. Four-night cruises booked last-minute cost from $1,000 per person.

Via Natura (CC Dicentro, 3rd Fl., Del Parque Oe7-154, tel. 2/600-5011, www.vianatura.com) offers cruise tours to the Galápagos on the first-class *Monserrat* yacht and land-based tours staying at the Casa Natura hotel in Puerto Ayora. Prices range $966 per person for a four-day land-based tour, $1,800 per person for a five-day cruise, and $2,700 per person for an eight-day cruise on the *Monserrat*.

Guayaquil

Guayaquil has quite a few travel agencies, but not nearly as many as Quito. For Galápagos and rainforest trips, prices are similar to Quito, although last-minute bargains can be harder to come by.

Canodros (Solar 10, Urb. Santa Leonor, tel. 4/228-5711, U.S. tel. 800/613-6026, fax 4/228-7651, www.canodros.com) has Galápagos cruises aboard the *Galápagos Explorer II:* four days from $2,200 per person and seven days from $3,270 per person, but there are frequent promotions.

Ecoventura (Central 300, Miraflores, tel. 4/220-7177 or 800/633-7972, www.ecoventura.com) offers cruises aboard the first-class vessels *Eric, Flamingo I,* and *Letty* as well as live-aboard diving trips on the *Galápagos Sky.* Eight-day cruises cost from $3,300 per person.

Galápagos Sub-Aqua (Orellana 211 at Panamá, tel. 4/230-5514, www.galapagos-sub-aqua.com) is one of the best diving operators in the Galápagos and offers a range of live-aboard cruises on the *Galápagos Aggressor, Humboldt Explorer,* and *Wolf and Darwin Buddy.* Eight-day live-aboard trips run $3,500-4,500 per person. There are also 5-8-day land-based tours, and day tours ($200 pp) that include two dives and the PADI training course.

Galasam (9 de Octubre 424 at Córdova, Ed. Gran Pasaje, tel. 4/230-4488, fax 4/231-1485, www.galasam.com.ec) offers tours on the deluxe-class *Queen of Galápagos,* the first-class *Estrella de Mar,* and the tourist-class *Amigo* as well as diving cruises on the *Humboldt Explorer.*

A four-day first-class cruise costs from $1,500 per person, eight-days from $2,900 per person. **Metropolitan Touring** (Calle 11 NE 103 and Av. 1 NE, Atarazana, tel./fax 4/228-4666) focuses on higher-end tours but has a huge range of cruises and land-based tours. The sales office is in the Hilton Colon in Kennedy. Four-day cruises cost from $1,500 per person, and eight-day cruises cost up to $4,935 per person. **Ninfa Tour** (Córdova 646 at Urdaneta, tel. 4/230-0182, www.galapagosninfatour.com) offers land-based tours staying at Hotel Ninfa in Puerto Ayora as well as island-hopping itineraries. Five-day tours cost from $400 per person.

The Galápagos Islands

Most visitors still arrive in the archipelago with their tour already arranged, but with the growing number of budget hotels and tour operators, you can make big savings by booking in Puerto Ayora. The low seasons in May-June and September-October are the best times to find cut-rate deals, but you may get lucky at any time of year. It's worth shopping around and hanging around for a few days to browse. Note that flexibility is usually essential to getting a good deal. The following operators are recommended for last-minute deals and day tours to surrounding islands such as Seymour Norte, the Plaza Islands, Bartolomé, Santa Fé, and Floreana. There are operators in Baquerizo Moreno and Puerto Villamil, but they are mainly restricted to offering day tours.

Galapatur (Rodríguez Lara and Genovesa, tel. 5/252-6088, www.galapatur.com) offers 4-8-day tours on the *Guantamera* and the *Yolita II,* and land-based tours from the new Galápagos Islands Hotel.

Galápagos Deep (Indefatigable and Matazarno, tel. 5/252-7045, www.galapagosdeep.com) offers day tours and diving courses.

Galápagos Sub-Aqua (Darwin, tel. 5/252-6350 and 5/252-6633, Guayaquil tel. 4/230-5514 or 4/230-5507, www.galapagos-sub-aqua.com), run by founder Fernando Zambrano, is the longest-running dive center on the islands, with 20 years of experience and a good safety record. The office in Puerto Ayora offers day dives for $200 per person, although last-minute discounts are available. Eight-day live-aboard trips range $3,500-4,500 per person.

Metropolitan Touring (Finch Bay Hotel, tel. 5/252-6297, www.metropolitan-touring.com) is the oldest operator in the islands with a big range of cruises and land-based itineraries at the Finch Bay Hotel.

Moonrise Travel (Darwin, tel. 5/252-6348, www.galapagosmoonrise.com) offers cruises, land-based tours, diving live-aboard cruises, and even camping in the Santa Cruz highlands.

Scuba Iguana (Darwin, tel. 5/252-6497, www.scubaiguana.com) is the other reputable operator, run by dive master Matías Espinosa, who was featured in the *Galápagos* IMAX movie. Daily dive rates are $200 per person. They also book live-aboard cruises for $3,500-4,500 per person.

We are the Champions Tours (Darwin, tel. 5/252-6951, www.wearethechampionstours.com) offers a wide range of cruises on 16 boats of all classes as well as hotel-based island-hopping tours and live-aboard cruises.

Recreation

DIVING

With such an astonishing array of marine life, it's no surprise that the Galápagos ranks among the world's best dive destinations. The New York Zoological Society's Oceanographic Expedition sent divers to the islands for the first time in 1925, and they've been returning ever since. In 1998 protection of the land sites was extended to a marine zone 74 kilometers offshore, and there are now some 60 dive sites around the archipelago, many of them closed to nondivers.

If you're dreaming of getting your PADI certification and heading straight here, however, be advised that diving in the Galápagos is not for beginners. Local dive schools offer PADI training, but it is overpriced and far from the best place to learn. You are better off not only learning elsewhere but getting a few dives under your belt first. Currents are strong, and visibility is often poor, ranging 10-25 meters (half that of the Caribbean). Many dives are in unsheltered water, meaning that holding onto coral is not only permitted but is essential. It is not ideal for the health of the coral, but it is certainly important for your health. There have been diving accidents here—some people get so excited by what they are seeing that they lose track of time and distance. Luckily, there is a decompression chamber in Puerto Ayora.

For those with sufficient experience, the diving is world-class. Schools of fish stretch out for what seems like eternity, and you're almost guaranteed close encounters with a variety of sharks—small white-tipped reef sharks, larger Galápagos sharks, the dramatically shaped hammerheads, and off the more remote western islands, enormous whale sharks. When you add to this extended periods following manta rays, marine iguanas, and the surprisingly fast penguins, the diving in the Red Sea or the Caribbean will pale in comparison.

Recent changes in the law mean that every boat in the Galápagos must be either a non-diving cruise boat or a dedicated dive boat, so divers are now forced to choose between live-aboard charters, which are very expensive, or a land-based tour with day trips to dive sites. The latter option is becoming more popular because it's far cheaper, but note that you will be restricted to sites within easy reach of Santa Cruz and San Cristóbal. Popular sites include Academy Bay, Santa Fé, Gordon Rocks, Daphne Minor, Mosquera, Seymour Norte, and Cousins.

However, the most spectacular diving can only be experienced on a live-aboard around Darwin and Wolf. These islands are a full day's sail north of the main island group. Schools of hundreds of hammerheads can be seen off Wolf, and gigantic whale sharks cruise slowly by June-November. Bottlenose dolphins are common at Darwin's Arch.

The best diving is during the hot season (Dec.-May), with 20-25°C water temperatures making a three-millimeter wetsuit adequate. Temperatures drop to 15°C in the cold season, when a six-millimeter wetsuit with hood, booties, and gloves becomes necessary. It's best to bring all your own equipment, as renting it locally is expensive and can cause problems because many itineraries go straight to the boat. Bring a mask, dive alert whistle, and sausage or scuba tuba. Boats supply tanks, air, and weights.

Because most visitors depart by plane, you must leave a day free at the end of your dive trip to avoid possible decompression problems (most dive tours spend the last day on Santa Cruz).

Dive Sites

For beginners, three sites around **Santa Fé** have moderate currents, and you can spot stingrays, turtles, sea lions, and reef sharks. Highlights include a large eel colony, sea lions, fur seals, golden eagle rays, and hammerheads. **Pinzón,** a small island between Santa Cruz and Isabela 1.5 hours from Puerto Ayora, has wall dives up to 30 meters for novices and intermediate level. **Seymour Norte** is also suitable for beginners, although there are also sites for more advanced divers. This is often combined with **Mosquera,** between Seymour Norte and Baltra, an intermediate wall dive with eels, turtles, rays, hammerheads, and barracudas. More difficult is the diving around the tuff cone of **Daphne Minor,** west of Baltra. This 90-foot wall dive contains strong currents. It's a good place to spot the Galápagos shark as well as rays and eels.

Farther north, there are several good sites around **Santiago.** The triangular-shaped **Cousins Rock** is the best known, with a fascinating series of ledges and overhangs and a vast range of species, including sharks, golden eagle rays, and fur seals. A tour here is often combined with nearby **Bartolomé,** where you can also snorkel with penguins. **Beagle Rocks** is also nearby, a relatively easy drift dive with a variety of tropical fish as well as sharks. Farther away on the northwest side of Santiago is a site at the protected cove of **Albany Rock,** where there are large groups of barracuda, sea lions, turtles, and sharks.

In the south, **Floreana** also has some excellent sites, although **Devil's Crown** is now closed to divers, and only snorkeling from cruises is permitted. The highlight here is a drift dive with sea lions at **Champion Island.** This is either combined with a dive at **Punta Cormorant,** suitable for beginners, or at **Enderby,** for more experienced divers.

San Cristóbal has great diving at the towering basalt monoliths of **Kicker Rock** (León Dormido), an excellent spot to see hammerheads, Galápagos sharks, and reef sharks. This trip is usually combined with Isla Lobos, where you can snorkel or dive among a large sea lion colony.

In the central region, **Gordon Rocks** (1 hour from Puerto Ayora) is recommended only for intermediate to advanced divers (with experience of 25-30 dives), and it is one of the most difficult sites. The visibility is often excellent, though, and there are opportunities to watch hammerhead sharks, a variety of rays, moray eels, and marine turtles.

Most of the other dive sites in the archipelago at Española, Isabela, and off Marchena can only be experienced on a live-aboard cruise. The most spectacular diving is around Darwin and Wolf, but this requires a minimum experience of 50-100 dives. These islands are a full day's sail north of the main island group. Schools of hundreds of hammerheads can be seen off Wolf, and gigantic whale sharks cruise slowly by between June and November. Bottlenose dolphins are common at Darwin's Arch.

Dive Operators

Choosing the right dive company is essential for your own safety. Most operators in Puerto Ayora and Baquerizo Moreno are reputable, but there are some who will take your money without asking questions. You are strongly advised to steer clear of any operator who doesn't ask you in detail about your experience. For example, any operator willing to take novices to Gordon Rocks should be avoided completely. The best operators ask you to fill out a detailed questionnaire to assess experience.

Most large Galápagos tour agencies can book dive trips aboard the small number of equipped boats. A PADI Open Water certificate is essential, and some companies ask for a minimum number of dives, although this depends on the difficulty of the site. A PADI Open Water

TRAVELS WITH CHARLIE

Nothing could be less inviting than the first appearance. A broken field of black basaltic lava, thrown into the most rugged waves and crossed by great fissures, is everywhere covered by stunted, sunburnt brushwood, which shows little signs of life.

Charles Darwin in *The Voyage of the Beagle*, unimpressed by his first glimpse of the Galápagos Islands

course generally costs around $450 per person for a four-day training course.

There are several reputable local dive specialists. **Galápagos Sub-Aqua** (Darwin, Puerto Ayora, tel. 5/252-6350 or 5/252-6633, Guayaquil tel. 4/230-5514 or 4/230-5507, www.galapagos-sub-aqua.com) is the longest-operating dive center on the islands, with 20 years of experience and a good safety record. Eight-day live-aboard trips ($3,500-4,500 pp) are offered, and day dives from Puerto Ayora cost $200 per person.

Other recommended operators in Puerto Ayora include **Scuba Iguana** (Darwin, tel. 5/252-6497, www.scubaiguana.com), run by dive master Matías Espinosa, who was featured in the *Galápagos* IMAX movie. Daily dive prices start at $200 per person. They also book live-aboard trips. **Nauti Diving** (Darwin, tel. 5/252-7004, www.nautidiving.com) and **Galápagos Deep** (Indefatigable and Matazarno, tel. 5/252-7045, www.galapagosdeep.com) run day trips.

Dive Tours

Live-aboard cruise options are very limited and are usually booked months in advance. At present, the two best companies are **Ecoventurer** (U.S. tel. 800/633-7972, Guayaquil tel. 4/283-9390, www.ecoventurer.com), operating the MY *Galápagos Sky,* and **Aggressor** (U.S. tel. 800/348-2628, www.aggressor.com), operating the *Galápagos Aggressor I* and *II.* Prices start around $3,800 per person, rising to $4,700 per person for a week.

SNORKELING

If diving is not for you, don't worry: The Galápagos also ranks as one of the world's best snorkeling destinations. Sea lions, marine turtles, stingrays, reef sharks, marine iguanas, flightless cormorants, and a vast array of tropical fish can all be seen at dozens of snorkeling sites throughout the archipelago. Most cruises and day tours include use of snorkels and fins, but you can also rent them from most operators in the ports, or bring your own. Some of the best snorkeling sites available on day trips include Isla Lobos and Kicker Rock (León Dormido) on San Cristóbal, Champion Island near Floreana, Bartolomé, and Las Tintoreras on Isabela. Travelers on cruises will have daily opportunities to snorkel at a wide variety of sites inaccessible to day tours.

Snorkeling Operators

All dive operators also offer snorkeling day trips. The best in Puerto Ayora are **Scuba Iguana** (Darwin, tel. 5/252-6497, www.scubaiguana.com) and **Galápagos Sub-Aqua** (Darwin, tel. 5/252-6350 or 5/252-6633, www.galapagos-sub-aqua.com). Other tour operators offering day trips include **Galápagos Voyager** (Darwin at Colon, tel. 5/252-6833), **Moonrise Travel** (Darwin, tel. 5/252-6348, www.galapagosmoonrise.com), **We are the Champions Tours** (Darwin, tel. 5/252-6951, www.wearethechampionstours.com), **Galapatur** (Rodríguez Lara and Genovesa, tel. 5/252-6088), and **Galápagos Deep** (Indefatigable and Matazarno, tel. 5/252-7045, www.

galapagosdeep.com). You can rent your own snorkeling guide to explore some of the nearby snorkeling sites at any of these operators.

SURFING

While it may seem a little odd to come to the world's top wildlife-watching destination and spend your time catching waves, the Galápagos is a popular place for surfers—mainly locals but some international surfers too. Recent restrictions have made surfing more difficult; the national park has closed some of the best spots to surfers, and others can be difficult to reach due to a lack of tours. The best time of year for surfing, as on the mainland, is December-May. The center of surfing in the archipelago is San Cristóbal, which has a few good sites within easy access of Baquerizo Moreno. The island picks up north and south Pacific swells on the northwest and southwest coasts. Punta Carola is the best north swell, a 10-minute boat ride from the port. El Cañon is also close to town. The best south swells are La Lobería and Tongo Reef. If you get a group together to do a day tour, a more remote spot is Manglecito near Kicker Rock (León Dormido). On Santa Cruz, there are a few beaches close to Puerto Ayora: La Ratonera and Bazán near Charles Darwin Station, along with Tortuga Bay. West of Puerto Ayora, there are good swells at Cerro Gallina and Las Palmas, although picking up tours to these sites can sometimes be difficult.

Surfing Rentals, Classes, and Tours

Most surfers bring their own gear, but you can rent boards from various operators. In Baquerizo Moreno, try **Dive and Surf Club** (Hernan Melville, tel. 8/087-7122 or 8/634-7256, www.divesurfclub.com), which offers a full day of surf classes at Puerto Chino for $70 per person. Other operators renting surfboards include **Sharksky** (Española, tel. 5/252-1188,

www.sharksky.com) and **Galakiwi** (Darwin, tel. 5/252-1562, www.galakiwi.com or www.southernexposuretours.co.nz). In Puerto Ayora, board rentals are more difficult to come by, and operators frequently open and close, so ask locally. A useful website based in mainland Ecuador is www.galapagosurf.net, which has detailed surfing information and occasional tours. A Quito-based operator, **Surf Galápagos** (Amazonas and Veintimilla, Quito, tel. 2/254-6028, www.surfgalapagos.com), also offers specialist surfing tours.

HIKING

Although much of your time in the Galápagos is spent either on the water or in the water, there are plenty of good hiking trails, most of which are strictly regulated. Most visitor sites have trails ranging from a few hundred meters to a few kilometers. However, many of them can be muddy or along uneven rocky routes, so make sure you come equipped with good walking shoes. In most cases, tennis shoes or sneakers are sufficient, but for longer hikes in the highlands, such as Sierra Negra on Isabela, walking boots are more advisable.

All three major ports have pleasant walks nearby. From Puerto Ayora there are short hikes to Las Grietas and Tortuga Bay. From Baquerizo Moreno there are walks to Frigate Bird Hill and La Lobería beach, and from Puerto Villamil there are hikes to the Tortoise Breeding Center and farther along to the Wall of Tears. Inland on Santa Cruz, more serious hikers can tackle the five-hour climb from Bellavista to Media Luna. On San Cristóbal, there is good hiking in the highlands around Laguna El Junco and at Punta Pitt. Isabela boasts perhaps the most famous hike on the islands, along the trail to Sierra Negra, the second largest volcanic crater in the world. There are two trails, one that takes four hours and a longer one that takes about seven hours.

THE GALÁPAGOS ISLANDS

The Galápagos comprises 13 volcanic islands and 16 tiny islets. The total population of the archipelago is 25,000, according to the 2010 census. Only four of the islands are populated: Santa Cruz, by far the largest with 15,000 people; San Cristóbal has 7,400; Isabela, 2,200; and Floreana, fewer than 200 people. These are the only islands that can be visited independently on shuttle ferry services. The populated areas account for only 3 percent of the archipelago's surface area, with the rest protected in the national park. There are 70 land visitor sites and roughly the same number of marine sites. Sites on Seymour Norte, Plaza Sur, Bartolomé, and Santa Fé can all be reached by either cruises or guided day trips from Santa Cruz. The other main islands in the archipelago—Española, Santiago, Rábida, Genovesa, Darwin, Wolf, the northern part of Isabela, and Fernandina—can only be visited on cruises. Pinta and Marchena in the north are both off-limits to visitors.

Santa Cruz and the surrounding islets receive the most visitors. San Cristóbal also gets busy in high season, and Isabela is just starting to expand as a tourism base. The more far-flung islands that are only accessible to cruises are much quieter. Whichever islands you visit, you can only see a tiny proportion of the archipelago: The 70 visitor sites represent only 0.01 percent of the total land mass, and the rest of the national park is strictly out-of-bounds to visitors.

Look for to find recommended dining and lodging on the islands.

© BEN WESTWOOD

Santa Cruz and Nearby Islands

Santa Cruz (pop. 15,000) is the economic, tourism, and geographic center of the Galápagos. It's the best base to explore surrounding islands on day tours and pick up last-minute deals. Many of the island's attractions can be seen independently, which is not the case in much of the rest of the archipelago.

Puerto Ayora is the archipelago's largest port and tourism hub with the widest selection of hotels and restaurants. On the edge of town is **Charles Darwin Research Station,** the most convenient place to view giant tortoises up close. A 45-minute walk west of Puerto Ayora is the sandy expanse of **Tortuga Bay,** the

longest beach in the Galápagos. Another short hike from town are the brackish waters of **Las Grietas,** fissures in the lava rocks that make for a relaxing cool dip. In the verdant highlands, there are several attractions that make an interesting day trip: **Los Gemelos** (the twins) are two 30-meter-deep craters with abundant birdlife. East of Bellavista are the **lava tunnels** formed by the solidified outer skin of a molten lava flow. The biggest highland attraction is the huge **El Chato Tortoise Reserve,** where these giants roam in their natural habitat. On the north side of the island, **Bachas Beach** is a frequent stop on tours to nearby Seymour

THE GALÁPAGOS ISLANDS

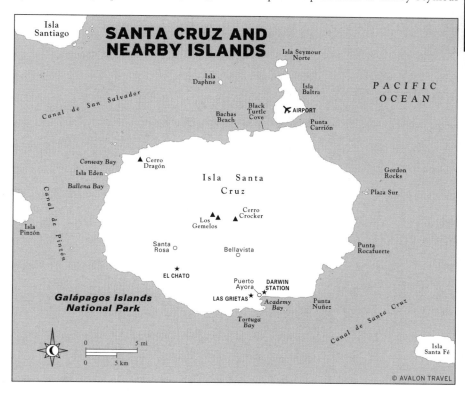

© AVALON TRAVEL

ISLAND NAMES

Most of the islands in the Galápagos have a Spanish name and an English name, and some even have three names. This is the legacy of both English and Spanish interest in the islands, whose ownership was not settled until Ecuador claimed them in 1832. Where possible, the Spanish name is used in this book, although some of the smaller islands have a sole English name. All are listed here alphabetically, followed by any variations. All names are official, except Floreana and Santiago, whose official names are Santa María and San Salvador.

- Baltra (South Seymour)
- Bartolomé (Bartholomew)
- Beagle
- Cowley
- Darwin (Culpepper)
- Enderby
- Española (Hood)
- Fernandina (Marlborough)
- Floreana (Charles)
- Genovesa (Tower)
- Isabela (Albemarle)
- Marchena (Bindloe)
- Pinta (Abingdon)
- Pinzón (Duncan)
- Plaza
- Rábida (Jervis)
- San Cristóbal (Chatham)
- Santa Cruz (Indefatigable)
- Santa Fé (Barrington)
- Santiago (James)
- Seymour Norte (North Seymour)
- Sin Nombre (Nameless)
- Tortuga (Brattle)
- Wolf (Wenman)

Norte, Plaza Sur, or on the way from the airport. The beach still contains the wreckage of U.S. military barges from World War II as well as populations of sally lightfoot crabs and flamingos in nearby lagoons. Less frequently visited are the lagoons of **Black Turtle Cove** and **Cerro Dragon.**

PUERTO AYORA AND VICINITY

If you're expecting to come to the Galápagos and stay in a deserted island paradise far from other humans, Puerto Ayora will come as something of a surprise. With a permanent population of about 12,000 and thousands more temporary residents and travelers, this is the bustling hub of the archipelago. While conservationists may wish the port away, blaming its expansion for the islands' environmental problems, it's hard to dislike Puerto Ayora. Set in a sheltered bay lined with cacti and filled with dozens of anchored yachts, it's a pleasant place to be based for a few days. The docks are particularly attractive, with a new jetty that is lit up at night. To the east near Banco del Pacífico is a small fish market that attracts dozens of pelicans and a small colony of sea lions looking for scraps that fishermen are happy to supply.

The facilities here are the best in the archipelago: hotels of all levels, from budget to seriously overpriced; a wide selection of good restaurants; reputable tour operators; and plenty of gift shops. If you're traveling independently, it makes most sense to stay here to pick up day tours or last-minute cruises.

However, note that Puerto Ayora has its drawbacks—there's too much traffic, especially the countless white-truck taxis shuttling around town. More serious are the problems with the water supply, and the construction of

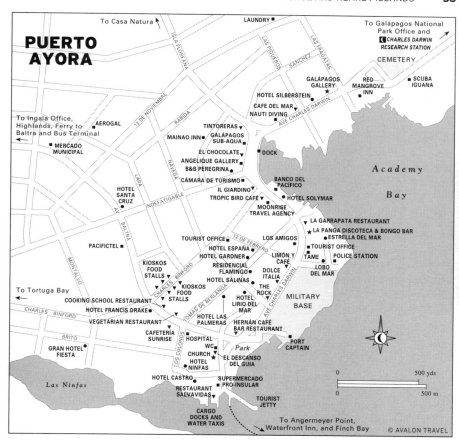

a decent sewage treatment facility is long over-due. The water supply here is dirtier than in mainland Ecuador (which is hardly a bench-mark)—so don't drink it, and use bottled water to clean your teeth.

Entertainment and Events

The downstairs disco **La Panga** (Darwin, 8 P.M.-2 A.M. daily) and upstairs bar **Bongo Bar** are the best places to have a big night out. La Panga often has a $10 cover charge on the weekend and pumps out mainly electronic music. There are a few mellower bars around

town to shoot pool and relax over a beer, nota-bly **Limón y Café** (Darwin and 12 de Febrero, 7 P.M.-2 A.M. daily). Otherwise most visitors simply linger in one of the many appealing wa-terfront restaurants for after-dinner drinks.

Shopping

You're never more than a few meters from a souvenir store in Puerto Ayora, and most sell postcards and the obligatory Galápagos-branded T-shirts and hats. Some stores also sell collectable stamps, handicrafts, wood-carvings, ceramics, and jewelry. The biggest concentration of stores is found along Darwin toward the Charles Darwin Center. Prices are reasonable by U.S. standards but inflated by Ecuadorian standards. Expect to pay about $10 for a T-shirt or hat, although some negotiating is possible. Some of the smaller stores a few blocks inland tend to be a bit cheaper because they receive less business. Note that you should steer clear of buying anything made of endangered black coral or turtle shells. For completely guilt-free shopping, the Charles Darwin Center has two gift shops whose profits go to the national park and the Darwin Foundation.

Stores a cut above the rest for more serious shoppers include **Galapagos Jewelry** (Darwin, www.galapagosjewelry.com) and **Luigi** (Darwin and Marchena, tel. 5/252-6868, www.luigigalapagos.com) for jewelry, **Olga Fisch** (Darwin and Seymour, tel. 2/254-1315, www.olgafisch.com) for rugs, tapestries, and other artisan wares, and **Galería Aymara** (Darwin and Los Piqueros, tel. 5/252-6835, www.galeria-aymara.com) for pottery, artwork, and jewelry. All are located on the east end of Avenida Darwin.

Recreation and Tours

Puerto Ayora is the best place to pick up day tours around Santa Cruz and to nearby islands. The cheapest tours are the bay tour ($35 pp), which takes in La Lobería, where you can snorkel with sea lions; Playa de los Perros, where marine iguanas and various birds are seen; Las Tintoreras, channels where sharks are often found; and the lava rock fissures of Las Grietas. The highlands tour goes to El Chato Tortoise Reserve, the nearby lava tunnels, and Los Gemelos collapsed craters. Alternatively, see many of these sights independently with a taxi driver for about $30 for a half-day.

For visits to nearby islands, the cheaper tours go to Floreana ($75 pp) and Santa Fé ($60 pp).

A pelican waits for scraps at the fish market in Puerto Ayora.

© CAROLINA WESTWOOD

The famed Galápagos tortoise Lonesome George, the last of his species, died in June 2012.

are a couple of kiosks opposite the dock). It can be a bumpy ride, particularly in the afternoon, so eat lightly beforehand or not at all.

White *camionetas* (pickup trucks) are available for hire around town, and most destinations cost $1, but it's better to walk or rent a bike. You can also negotiate taxi prices to go into the highlands (usually $30 for a half-day). **Water taxis** wait at the dock to shuttle passengers to boats waiting in the harbor ($0.60 pp by day, $1 at night) and across to the dock of Angermeyer Point to reach Playa de los Alemanes and Las Grietas.

If you're in a hurry and can spare the extra cost, take an interisland flight with **Emetebe** (Los Colonos and Darwin, top Fl., tel. 5/252-6177). Small eight-seat planes fly half-hour routes among San Cristóbal, Baltra, and Isabela several times per week. Fares start at $160 one-way, $260 round-trip, plus $15 taxes. Other airline offices in town are **TAME** (Darwin and 12 de Febrero, tel. 5/252-6527), **AeroGal**

(Rodríguez Lara and San Cristóbal, tel. 5/244-1950), and **LAN** (Darwin, www.lan.com.ec).

Charles Darwin Research Station

About 15 minutes' walk east of town is the headquarters of the Charles Darwin Foundation (tel. 5/252-6146, www.darwinfoundation.org, 7 A.M.-6 P.M. daily). The station was opened in the 1960s as a research and breeding center for endangered native species. Note that it's not very well signposted. The first office on the left is the national park's headquarters. Keep walking and take the next path left to reach a small exhibition at the **Van Straelen Visitors Center.** The main attraction is the **Tortoise Breeding Center Fausto Llerena,** where endangered subspecies are hatched and cared for until they can be released into the wild. There are also some land iguanas in enclosures farther along, but the highlight of the visit is the set of giant tortoise enclosures, where you can meet these amazing creatures face to face. These used to be walk-in enclosures where you could walk among the tortoises, but the national park has recently closed them, so you must be content with viewing them over the short walls. There are now 10 different subspecies. The most famous resident was **Lonesome George,** the last surviving member of the Pinta Island subspecies. He died in June 2012.

Note that the station is on almost every tour itinerary, so it's a good idea to get here early to avoid the crowds. A small beach just outside the station is open 7 A.M.-6 P.M. daily.

Tortuga Bay

Galápagos tours can have hectic schedules, so you may welcome the chance to lie on a pristine beach for a few hours. Luckily, one of the most beautiful beaches in the Galápagos is only a 45-minute walk from Puerto Ayora. Take Binford out of town to the west, up the steps, and past the national park guard

post, where you need to sign in and where you can buy refreshments. Follow the paved path through cacti forest 2.5 kilometers to the beach. Finches and a variety of birds can be seen along the path. Unfortunately, the path is also sometimes plagued by an invasive species of wasps, so take care. At the end of the path is a spectacular beach, **Playa Brava,** one of the longest in the archipelago. Note that the sea is a rough here, so it's good for surfers but usually dangerous for swimmers. For a gentle soak, walk along to the right to the very end of the beach and turn inland past a group of marine iguanas to find a smaller shallow lagoon and **Playa Mansa,** where marine turtles come to lay their eggs. You're unlikely to see the turtles, so content yourself with sunbathing and swimming in this idyllic spot. Note that the beach closes at 5 P.M., so you should set out earlier than 3 P.M. to have enough time to enjoy it. There are no facilities, so bring

the sheltered lagoon of Playa Mansa, Tortuga Bay

© CAROLINA WESTWOOD

© BEN WESTWOOD

Relax at Las Grietas with a relaxing dip in the brackish waters.

water and refreshments, and be sure to take the trash back with you.

Las Grietas

Another nearby excursion within walking distance of the port is Las Grietas, where fissures in the lava rocks have created two layers of brackish water—saline and fresh. Take a water taxi ($0.60) across the bay to the dock of Angermeyer Point restaurant and walk past the Finch Bay Hotel to Playa de los Alemanes (German Beach), a small sandy beach. Then walk up a path strewn with lava rocks to the steps leading down to Las Grietas. The hike from the dock takes about half an hour, and good walking shoes are preferable for the rocky parts. Note that the descent, clambering down rocks to the water, is particularly tricky for elderly people or small children. It's a beautiful, sheltered place for a refreshing swim, though, but come early to avoid the crowds.

SANTA CRUZ HIGHLANDS

The Galápagos's reputation for barren landscapes certainly doesn't apply to the highlands of Santa Cruz, and it's worth venturing inland and up 600 meters to experience a very different environment than the coast—misty forests and green pastures. Seven kilometers above Puerto Ayora are the small towns of **Bellavista** and **Santa Rosa,** from which several trails lead into the hills. The peaks of **Media Luna,** five kilometers from Bellavista, can be climbed in 4-5 hours, and three kilometers beyond them is **Cerro Crocker,** a journey of 7-8 hours. Having a guide is advised but not required.

West of Santa Rosa, the biggest draw of the highlands is **El Chato Tortoise Reserve** ($3), which fills the entire southwest corner of the island. Here you can see the giants in their natural habitat on guided hikes through the forest. There's a slightly dubious photo opportunity at the end of the tour, where visitors can wear the heavy shell of a dead tortoise.

A few kilometers up from Santa Rosa on either side of the road are **Los Gemelos,** 30-meter-deep craters formed when caverns left empty by flowing lava collapsed on themselves. The view is impressive into the now verdant craters, where Galápagos hawks, barn owls, and vermillion flycatchers flit through damp *Scalesia* forests.

East of Bellavista, you can visit two sets of **lava tunnels** ($3), formed by the solidified outer skin of a molten lava flow. Entered through collapsed roof sections, the wide tunnels feel like mine shafts and stretch for nearly one kilometer. It's quite wet and muddy, so sneakers are preferable to sandals. The tunnels are on private land.

Steve Devine's Butterfly Farm ($4), between Bellavista and Santa Rosa, is another popular stop on tours of the highlands. This cattle ranch is run by a former American GI. Giant tortoises graze in the wet grass among the cattle, and there are abundant butterflies and birds, including yellow warblers and vermillion flycatchers. There's a restaurant and café if you want to stop for lunch.

All of the attractions above can be seen on a guided tour organized with any operator in Santa Cruz. Costs average $80 total, shared among groups of up to 14. Alternatively, pay a taxi driver in the port about $30 for a half day to see some of the attractions yourself.

OTHER SANTA CRUZ VISITOR SITES
Bachas Beach
This beach is named for the remains of U.S. military barges wrecked during World War II; the rusty metal parts are still visible jutting out of the sand. The white-sand beach is often covered in sally lightfoot crabs and is also a sea turtle nesting site, while the lagoons behind the beach are home to flamingos. Las Bachas is often combined with other excursions such as Seymour Norte, or it can be seen on the way to or from the airport due to its proximity to Baltra.

Black Turtle Cove
Just west of the canal between Santa Cruz and Baltra, this shallow mangrove lagoon extends far inland. There is no landing site, so visitors are restricted to a slow tour on a *panga* (small boat). Above water, there is abundant birdlife: herons, gulls, frigate birds, and boobies all nest in the tangled branches of red and white mangroves. Beneath the surface, golden and spotted eagle rays glide by, and green sea turtles are often seen mating September-February. You may also be lucky enough to see white-tipped sharks resting in the shallows. This site is often included at the beginning or end of tours due to its proximity to the airport on Baltra.

Cerro Dragon (Dragon Hill)
This new visitor site on the west side of the island has a dry or wet landing, depending on the tide. There are two lagoons that are sometimes filled with flamingos, and a two-kilometer trail through a forest of *palo santo* and opuntia cacti leads to the top of Cerro Dragon, which commands good views. This is a good spot to see groups of land iguanas, which gave the hill its name, although most of them have been repatriated from Charles Darwin Research Station.

DAPHNE MAJOR
Off the north coast of Santa Cruz, about 10 kilometers west of Seymour Norte, the two small Daphne Islands are not included on most itineraries, and access is restricted. The larger island, Daphne Major, is an important research site. This is where Peter and Rosemary Grant researched finches, documented in the Pulitzer Prize-winning book *The Beak of the Finch* by Jonathon Weiner. If you can get permission to come here, and negotiate a very tricky landing, there is a steep trail to the 120-meter-high summit of a sunken crater, where masked and blue-footed boobies nest. Farther along the trail, red-billed tropic birds can also be seen.

SANTA FÉ
This small island is midway between Santa Cruz and San Cristóbal, about two hours from each. Landing on the island has recently been restricted to cruise tours. There's a wet landing on the northeast side and trails through a forest of opuntia cacti, which grow up to 10 meters high. The trail is rocky in places, and you have to cross a steep ravine, so bring good walking shoes. The highlight is the yellowish Santa Fé iguana, endemic to the island, and you may be lucky enough to see Galápagos hawks in the forest. On day tours (about $60 pp) you are not allowed to land, so the highlight is the snorkeling—marine turtles, manta rays, white-tipped reef sharks, and sea lions can be seen in the shallow waters. Take care, as some of the sea lion bulls can be bad-tempered. This island is

© JAVARMAN JAVARMAN/123RF

Blue-footed boobies have an entertaining mating ritual.

also a good diving spot, with three sites ranging from beginner to intermediate.

SEYMOUR NORTE

This tiny island off the north coast of Santa Cruz is the best place to see large colonies of blue-footed boobies and magnificent frigate birds. You can decide for yourself which has the most interesting mating ritual: the boobies marching around displaying their blue feet, or the frigates inflating their red chests to the size of a basketball. Both present great photo opportunities. After a slightly tricky dry landing on some rocks, the 2.5-kilometer trail loops around the island and takes over an hour. At the end, you can appreciate the amazing sight of marine iguanas, sea lions, and red sally lightfoot crabs sharing the rocky beaches. Offshore there is a good swell, and sometimes you can see the sea lions body-surfing. Note that this is a very popular island and gets rather crowded, so the national park

has raised the price of day trips from Puerto Ayora (about $125 pp). The diving around Seymour Norte is particularly good.

PLAZA SUR

Off the east coast of Santa Cruz are the two tiny Plaza Islands. You can only visit the south island, Plaza Sur, one of the smallest visitor sites in the archipelago at just two square kilometers. However, the island boasts one of the largest sea lion colonies in the Galápagos, with about 1,000 individuals, and it's a great place to observe a colony up close. It's fascinating to watch them lounging around, yawning, and tending to their young. Keep your distance from the large males, though, as they can get very irritable, and mothers suckling pups are understandably defensive at times.

The dry landing onto the docks usually includes a welcoming party of negligently stretched-out sea lions. A trail climbs through colorful landscape past a small colony of land iguanas to the far side of the island, where the cliffs teem with birdlife—red-billed tropic birds, boobies, frigates, and swallow-tailed gulls. The presence of both land and marine iguanas has led to a small hybrid colony, the offspring of both species mating. Like most hybrids, they are sterile. There is also a small sea lion bachelor colony,

separated from the main colony, plotting their next challenge to the dominant males below. Note that swimming or snorkeling here is not risk-free and most tours avoid it due to the aggression of sea lion bulls. Like Seymour Norte, Plaza Sur is a busy visitor site, and prices have been raised to $125 per person for day tours.

San Cristóbal

The most easterly island in the Galápagos, San Cristóbal is the administrative center and its port, Baquerizo Moreno, is the capital. It's not nearly as busy as Santa Cruz, and while Puerto Ayora has boomed in recent years, Baquerizo Moreno is a more modest tourism hub and very quiet off-season. However, San Cristóbal is leading the way in the archipelago's renewable energy drive, with 60 percent of its energy coming from wind and solar power, and the island authorities hope to eliminate diesel completely in the next five years. Its quiet vibe belies a troubled history, however; in the late 19th century it was the site of a large penal colony, inland at the small town of El Progreso. These days it's a pleasant enough place, with an excellent boat trip into the national park, excursions into the highlands, and walks to nearby beaches. However, unlike Santa Cruz, you can't really fill more than three days here.

Near Baquerizo Moreno are several short walks to interesting sites. Northeast of the center is **The Interpretation Center,** which has arguably the best exhibition in the archipelago on the islands' history and ecology. Beyond this are walks to **Las Tijeretas,** renowned for frigate birds, and **Playa Cabo de Horno,** a good spot for snorkeling. On the opposite side of town is a large sea lion colony at **La Lobería.**

Farther afield, the only marine day trip available takes in **Isla Lobos, Kicker Rock (León Dormido), Cerro Brujo,** and **Puerto Grande.**

At the northeast end of the island, **Punta Pitt** has large colonies of red-footed, blue-footed, and masked boobies. In the highlands, an interesting day trip takes in the freshwater lake **Laguna El Junco,** the large giant tortoise reserve of **La Galapaguera,** and the beach of **Puerto Chino.**

PUERTO BAQUERIZO MORENO

The capital of the Galápagos Islands has a different feel to Puerto Ayora in Santa Cruz. It's smaller, cheaper, and not completely dependent on tourism—fishing and administration are also important employment sources in the town. The port has a very pleasant waterfront walkway where sea lions lounge lazily, and the beach just west of the center is the sleeping area for an entire colony—dozens of them congregate here at night.

Sights

Baquerizo Moreno has several sights that can be visited independently within walking distance. A 10-minute walk north-east of the center along Alsacio Northia is the small, popular **Mann Beach,** which gets busy on the weekend. Note that the water is not particularly clean. Opposite the beach is a branch of the University of San Francisco de Quito, and students are frequent visitors to the beach.

Walk a little farther up to reach the

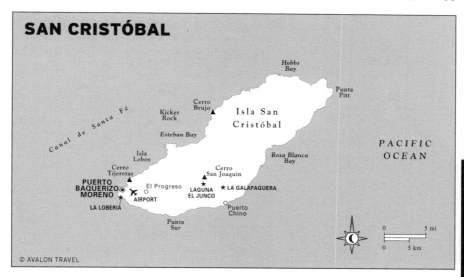

SAN CRISTÓBAL

Hobbs Bay

Punta Pitt

Cerro Brujo ▲

Kicker Rock

Esteban Bay

Isla San Cristóbal

Canal de Santa Fé

Isla Lobos

Cerro Tijeretas

PUERTO BAQUERIZO MORENO ◉

El Progreso ○

✈ **AIRPORT**

LAGUNA EL JUNCO ★

Cerro San Joaquin ▲

★ **LA GALAPAGUERA**

LA LOBERÍA ★

Punta Sur

○ *Puerto Chino*

Rosa Blanca Bay

PACIFIC OCEAN

0   5 mi
0   5 km

© AVALON TRAVEL

Interpretation Center (tel. 5/252-0358, 8 A.M.-5 P.M. daily, free), which provides an in-depth overview of the islands' history, development, and environmental problems. It's better than the smaller exhibition at the Charles Darwin Center in Puerto Ayora.

Past the center, there is a forked path leading up to **Las Tijeretas,** also known as **Frigate Bird Hill** for its abundance of nesting frigates. The views are very impressive to the bay below, which is a good spot for snorkeling, although the entry via the rocks can be a bit tricky. The other path leads down to **Playa Cabo de Horno,** also known as Playa de Amor, which has equally good snorkeling and a quiet stretch of beach, frequented by sea lions and backed by mangroves.

On the opposite end of town is **La Lobería,** a rocky beach where a large colony of sea lions laze around. It's 30 minutes' walk along the road but not exactly pleasant, so it's better to take a taxi ($2). Arrange a pickup time or walk back; expect to spend an hour or two here. This is the only place on the island where you can walk among a sea lion colony, and there are

usually dozens of them stretched out on the beach and rocks. There's a 600-meter trail parallel to the beach along which you can see marine iguanas. It's also a popular spot for surfers, but snorkeling is not recommended because of the currents.

Entertainment

Baquerizo Moreno comes alive at night, and you may be astonished at how many children and teenagers fill the waterfront on weekends. Nightlife options are restricted, though. The best place to go at night is three blocks inland at **Iguana Rock** (José Flores and Quito, 8 P.M.-2 A.M. Mon.-Sat.) where you can shoot pool and dance. There are various impromptu discos inland away from the center of town on the weekend. Just ask around, or watch for flyers. For a quieter evening, have a cocktail or beer at the waterfront **Casa Blanca Café** (Darwin, no phone, 8 A.M.-10 P.M. daily).

Recreation and Tours

The boat trip to **Isla Lobos** and **Kicker Rock (León Dormido)** is one of the best day trips

TRAVELS WITH CHARLIE

The inhabitants believe that these animals are absolutely deaf; certainly they do not overhear a person walking close behind them. I was always amused when overtaking one of these great monsters, as it was quietly pacing along, to see how suddenly, the instant I passed, it would draw in its head and legs, and uttering a deep hiss, fall to the ground with a heavy sound as if struck dead. I frequently got on their backs, and then giving a few raps on the hinder part of their shells, they would rise up and walk away, but I found it very difficult to keep my balance.

Charles Darwin in *The Voyage of the Beagle,* misbehaving with giant tortoises on his 1835 trip to the Galápagos

available on the archipelago and can be booked with most tour operators in town. Most are either on Avenida Darwin on the waterfront or along Española. You can also rent snorkeling gear, surfboards, and bicycles to get around. Recommended operators include **Sharksky** (Española, tel. 5/252-1188, www.sharksky. com), **Chalo's Tours** (Española, tel. 5/252-0953, chalotours@hotmail.com), and **Galakiwi** (Darwin, tel. 5/252-1562, www.galakiwi.com or www.southernexposuretours.co.nz). The trip to Kicker Rock and Isla Lobos costs $60 per person, and a day tour of the highlands costs $60 total, shared among a small group; you can do it yourself and hire a taxi to save money (about $30, or $10 per hour).

For scuba diving, all of the operators above organize tours, often on the same boats as snorkeling tours, or head to the **Dive and Surf Club** (Melville, tel. 9/409-5450, www.dive-surfclub.com). Diving at Kicker Rock and Isla Lobos costs $120 per person.

Accommodations

Baquerizo Moreno has fewer accommodations than Puerto Ayora, but there are plenty of budget options. It lacks a large selection of top-end hotels, which is not necessarily a bad thing because tour groups prefer to stay in Santa Cruz, keeping San Cristóbal quieter.

Along the *malecón* (beachfront road), the cheapest options offer basic guest rooms with private baths and fans. These include **Hostal San Francisco** (Malecón, tel. 5/252-0304, $10-12 pp) and **Hostal Albatross** (tel. 5/252-0264, $10 pp) right next door. For a little more money, a far better option is the family-run **Hostal León Dormido** (Jose de Villamil and Malecón, tel. 5/252-0169, $20 pp), which has well-maintained guest rooms with private baths, fans, and TVs, a cozy lounge area, and a small coffee shop downstairs.

For more comfort, try the air-conditioned waterfront rooms of **Suites Bellavista** (Malecón and Melville, tel. 5/252-0352, $50 s or d). Some guest rooms have great views of the harbor. The most elegant place to stay on the waterfront without breaking the bank is the Moorish white **Casa Blanca** (Malecón and Melville, tel. 5/252-0392, www.casablanca-galapagos.com, $30 s, $50 d), which has rustic guest rooms with air-conditioning, wide balconies with great views of the harbor, and an art gallery downstairs.

Inland, another good mid-range option is the friendly **Los Cactus** (Juan José Flores and Quito, tel. 5/252-0078, $25 s, $35 d, breakfast included). There are 13 guest rooms with private baths, hot water, air-conditioning, TVs, and Wi-Fi. On the road to the airport the remodeled **Hotel Chatham** (Northia and Armada Nacional, tel. 5/252-0137,

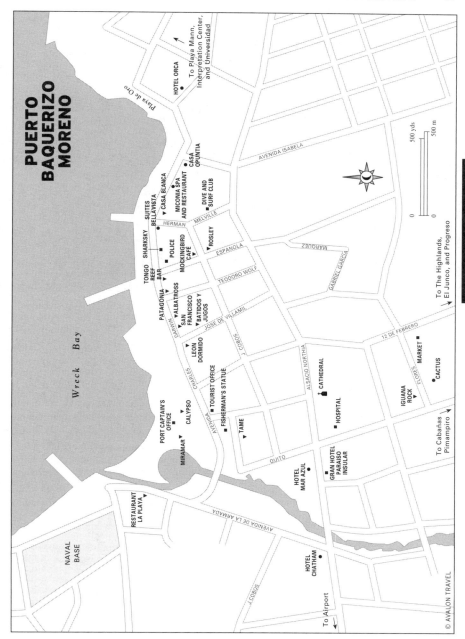

THE GALÁPAGOS ISLANDS

PUERTO
BAQUERIZO
MORENO

Wreck Bay

Playa de Oro

To Playa Mann,
Interpretation Center,
and Universidad

HOTEL ORCA

AVENIDA ISABELA

CASA
OPUNTIA

CASA BLANCA

MICONIA SPA
AND RESTAURANT

DIVE AND
SURF CLUB

SUITES
BELLAVISTA

HERMAN

MELVILLE

TONGO
REEF
BAR

SHARKSKY

POLICE

MOCKINGBIRD
CAFÉ

ROSLEY

ESPAÑOLA

MARQUEZ

PATAGONIA

ALBATROSS

SAN
FRANCISCO

BATIDOS Y
JUGOS

JOSE DE VILLAMIL

TEODORO WOLF

GABRIEL GARCIA

DARWIN

LEON
DORMIDO

COBOS

To The Highlands,
El Junco, and Progreso

CHARLES

TOURIST OFFICE

FISHERMAN'S STATUE

CATHEDRAL

ALSACIO NORTHIA

12 DE FEBRERO

FLORES

MARKET

CACTUS

IGUANA
ROCK

PORT CAPTAIN'S
OFFICE

CALYPSO

TAME

HOSPITAL

MIRAMAR

AVENIDA

QUITO

To Cabañas
Pimampiro

RESTAURANT
LA PLAYA

HOTEL
MAR AZUL

GRAN HOTEL
PARAISO
INSULAR

AVENIDA DE LA ARMADA

NAVAL
BASE

HOTEL
CHATHAM

COBOS

To Airport

500 yds

500 m

0

0

© AVALON TRAVEL

© CAROLINA WESTWOOD

sea lion on Baquerizo Moreno

chathamhotel@hotmail.com, $42 s, $72 d, breakfast included) has rooms with air-conditioning, hot water, TVs, and private baths along with a small pool. The guest rooms are also good at **Gran Hotel Paraíso Insular** (Northia and Esmeraldas, tel. 5/252-0091, www.grandhotelparaisoinsular.com, $40-60 s, $60-80 d), although the hotel is not quite as upmarket as its name suggests. Opposite, cheaper rooms with air-conditioning, cable TV, and private baths can be found at the **Hotel Mar Azul** (Northia and Esmeraldas, tel. 5/252-0139, $33 s or d).

The port has a few top-end hotels, but not as many as Puerto Ayora. **Miconia** (Darwin, tel. 5/252-0608, www.miconia.com, $87 s, $161 d), along the north end of the *malecón,* is one of the best. There's a pool, a jetted tub, a gym and Wi-Fi. The restaurant has a good reputation and is open to nonguests. Farther along, find a more intimate atmosphere at **Casa Opuntia** (Darwin, tel. 2/604-6800 in Quito, www.opuntiagalapagoshotels.com, $116 s, $147 d,

breakfast included) with 11 guest rooms above a terrace overlooking the harbor.

Food

There are plenty of cafés along the waterfront on Darwin that offer breakfasts, sandwiches, burgers, and snacks. These include **Patagonia** (tel. 5/252-0017, breakfast, lunch, and dinner daily, $2-5) and **Tongo Reef Bar** (tel. 5/252-1852, breakfast, lunch, and dinner daily, $2-5). A better option is **Casa Blanca Cafe** (no phone, breakfast, lunch, and dinner daily, $2-5), which also serves up traditional dishes such as tamales or *humitas* (mashed corn filled with chicken, vegetables, or cheese) as well as a wide range of cocktails and juices. Another good place for fresh juices and snacks is **Batidos y Jugos Mi Grande** (Jose de Villamil, tel. 5/252-0973, 6 A.M.-10 P.M. daily, $1.50-3).

If you want something more filling, it can be surprisingly difficult to find a good budget meal, and many restaurants do not advertise set menus. **Rosley** (Española and Hernández, no phone, lunch and dinner daily, entrées $3) is probably the best set-meal joint in town, serving up an excellent-value two-course lunch and dinner, and it is popular with locals. Opposite, the **Mockingbird Café** (Española and Hernández, tel. 5/252-0092, breakfast, lunch, and dinner daily, entrées from $2.50) is a good place to check your email accompanied by a coffee, milk shake, or brownie. **Rosita** (Villamil and Hernández, tel. 5/252-1581, breakfast, lunch, and dinner daily, entrées $10-15) has expensive fish, shellfish, and meat dishes on the menu but also offers a set meal for $4 (you have to ask for it).

If you don't mind spending upward of $10 on dinner, there are plenty of upscale options in town, mainly at the west end of the *malecón*. One of the most popular is **◖ La Playa** (Armada Nacional, tel. 5/252-0044, lunch and dinner daily, entrées $7-12), which specializes in mouthwatering seafood dishes such as ceviche and breaded sea bass. Nearby is the more formal **Miramar** (Darwin, 6-11 P.M. daily, entrées $10-18) with views worthy of its name. Its location, right next to a beach filled with snoozing sea lions, is ideal, and the menu has a wide range of international and seafood dishes, including fish in coconut sauce, and a long list of cocktails. The restaurant at **Hotel Miconia** (Darwin, tel. 5/252-0608, breakfast, lunch, and dinner daily, entrées $10) is also a good upscale option. Italian pizza and pasta are the main specialties, but the fried fish is also good.

Information and Services

The **CAPTURGAL** tourist information office (Hernández, tel. 5/252-1124) and the **Municipal tourist office** (Darwin and 12 de Febrero, tel. 5/252-0119 or 5/252-0358) are both open 8 A.M.-noon and 2-5 P.M. Monday-Friday. Telephone cabins can be found at several locations. Internet access can be found at the **Mockingbird Café** (Española and Hernández,

tel. 5/252-0092) and at several offices along the waterfront. Other services in town are the **post office,** at the western end of Darwin, past the municipal building; the **police station** (Darwin and Española, tel. 5/252-0101); and the town's main **hospital** (Northia and Quito, tel. 5/252-0118).

Getting There and Around

San Cristóbal's **airport** is at the end of Avenida Alsacio Northia past the radio station. Take a taxi ($2) from the airport to town. **Buses** leave from the *malecón* half a dozen times daily for El Progreso in the highlands, or take a **taxi** (about $3). The interisland boat service departs at 7 A.M. each morning for Santa Cruz (2 hours, $25 pp); for Isabela, continue from Santa Cruz at 2:30 P.M. (2.5 hours, $25 pp).

Emetebe (tel./fax 5/252-0615) has flights leaving most mornings at 8 A.M. for Baltra (30 minutes, $160 pp one-way) and Isabela (45 minutes, $160 pp).

MARINE SITES

San Cristóbal has some excellent marine sites, and most are reachable on day trips from Baquerizo Moreno. They are usually quieter than many of the sites visited from Puerto Ayora because fewer visitors base themselves on San Cristóbal. Playa del Amor and La Lobería can be visited independently, but the best marine sites require a boat trip.

Isla Lobos and Kicker Rock (León Dormido)

Isla Lobos is a tiny rocky island 30 minutes north of Baquerizo Moreno by boat. Walking on the island is prohibited, so just jump straight in for excellent snorkeling with sea lions in the channel between the islet and the shore. Boobies and frigates can also be seen nesting here. This site is combined with one of the Galápagos's most famous landmarks, **Kicker Rock,** also known as León Dormido (Sleeping

© BEN WESTWOOD

Kicker Rock, also known as León Dormido, is an excellent spot to snorkel with sharks.

Lion). Some people think it looks like a foot, while others see the shape of a lion. Whichever name you prefer, this is one of the best snorkeling and dive sites in the archipelago. The sheer-walled volcanic tuff cone has been eroded in half with a narrow channel between. This is a prime spot to spot sharks—white-tipped reef sharks are commonly seen in and around the channel, while divers can go deeper to see awesome schools of hammerheads. Sea turtles and a wide range of rays are also common. Boats are not allowed in the channel, waiting at either end while you snorkel or dive. Day trips usually stop afterward at the long white beach of **Cerro Brujo,** a beautiful coral sand beach ideal for more relaxed swimming, snorkeling, and sunbathing.

Punta Pitt

On the northeast tip of San Cristóbal, the farthest site from the port is Punta Pitt, which can now only be visited by cruise boats. A wet landing is followed by a long and fairly strenuous hike (two hours round-trip) past an olivine beach through thorny scrub and past tuff cones. The rewards are panoramic views and, more importantly, the only red-footed booby colony in the archipelago outside Genovesa, and the only spot where you can see all three booby species together. There are also populations of frigate birds, storm petrels, and swallow-tailed gulls. From here you can continue hiking for about two hours to reach the giant tortoise reserve at La Galapaguera.

SAN CRISTÓBAL HIGHLANDS

Avenida 12 de Febrero climbs north out of Baquerizo Moreno to El Progreso, a notorious former penal colony that's now a quiet farming village. There's not much to see, but for a unique experience, visit the **Casa del Ceibo** (near the main street, tel. 5/252-0248, $15 pp), a small house in a huge kapok tree. A maximum of two people can stay overnight.

Tracks continue north to the settlement of Soledad, near an overlook at the south end of the island, and east to Cerro Verde and Los Arroyos. About 10 kilometers east of Progreso on the way to Cerro Verde is a turn-off to the right along a steep dirt track to the **Laguna El Junco,** one of the few freshwater lakes in the Galápagos. At 700 meters above sea level, the collapsed caldera is fed by rainwater and shelters wading birds, frigates, the Chatham mockingbird, and seven species of Darwin's finches. It's also a good place to observe typical highland tree ferns. A narrow trail encircles the rim with spectacular panoramic views. Note that this site can get very muddy in the rainy season (Jan.-Apr.).

The road from Cerro Verde continues across the island to **Puerto Chino,** an isolated beach on the south coast. It's possible to camp here with permission from the national park office in the port.

A few kilometers inland from Puerto Chino is **La Galapaguera,** a giant tortoise reserve where San Cristóbal tortoises reside in 12 hectares of dry forest.

Most of the sights above can be visited on a guided tour ($50 pp), or save money by sharing a taxi (from $10 per hour).

Santiago and Nearby Islands

SANTIAGO

Stepping onto the Galápagos's fourth-largest island, also known as San Salvador, is rather like stepping back to the beginning of time. The effects of a long history of volcanic eruptions are everywhere on this island: Blackened lava dominates the landscape, and small plants and cacti are the first signs of life sprouting from the ashes. In recent years destruction of a different kind has occurred on the island. Feral goats, introduced in the 1880s, grew to number over 100,000 in less than a century. A large-scale effort by the Park Service and Charles Darwin Research Center successfully eradicated the goats by 2006. Santiago cannot be visited on day trips at present and must be visited as part of a cruise tour.

The most popular sites on and near Santiago include the black lava trails of **Sullivan Bay;** the colonies of sea lions, seals, and marine iguanas at **James Bay;** the famous **Pinnacle Rock** on Bartolomé, the most photographed site in the archipelago; and the bachelor sea lion colony and pelicans on **Rábida** Island. There are good diving spots at **Cousins Rock** and **Beagle Rocks** on the southeast side and at **Albany Rock** on the northwest side of the island.

Sullivan Bay

One of the most popular sites on the island is this bay on the east side. An eruption in 1897 left the area covered in mesmerizing patterns of black lava, known as *pahoehoe* (a Hawaiian word for rope) because of its tendency to buckle when it cools. The lava's glassy, almost ceramic feel comes from its high silicate content. The walk over 1.5 kilometers takes about 1.5 hours and is very uneven—it's a natural trail—so bring good walking shoes.

Buccaneer Cove

A freshwater source made this cove a haven for pirates in the 17th and 18th centuries. A few years back, divers found evidence in the form of ceramic jars on the seabed, still intact and filled with wine and marmalade. Few tours stop here, but many boats sail slowly past to allow passengers to appreciate the steep cliffs and dark-red volcanic sand beach.

THE GALÁPAGOS ISLANDS

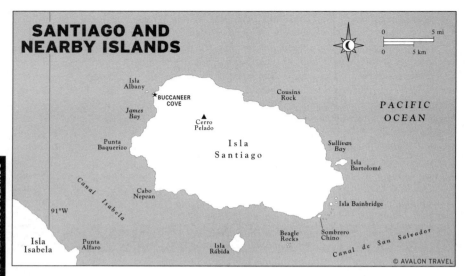

James Bay

On the west side of Santiago, a very popular visitor site is **Puerto Egas,** named after the owner of a salt mine that operated on the island in the 1960s. There is a wet landing onto the long black-lava shoreline, home to a small colony of sea lions and large populations of marine iguanas.

A two-kilometer, three-hour loop trail leads inland past the rusted remains of the salt mine and a rather makeshift soccer field built by cruise crews. Look to the skies and you may be lucky enough to see Galápagos hawks, circling in search of prey in the form of Galápagos doves and mockingbirds.

Farther down the trail are the famous fur-seal grottoes, where the ocean fills a series of pools and underwater caverns occupied by seals, sea lions, and bright-red sally lightfoot crabs. There are great snorkeling opportunities here.

A second, lesser-used path, frequented by Darwin's finches and Galápagos doves, rises 300 meters to **Sugarloaf Volcano.** It takes over an hour round-trip.

At the north end of James Bay, five kilometers from Puerto Egas, is **Espumilla Beach,** another good spot for swimming and snorkeling. Visitors make a wet landing onto a beach where sea turtles can sometimes be spotted; they come ashore at night to lay their eggs. A two-kilometer trail leads inland through the mangroves to a lagoon populated by Galápagos flamingos, herons, and other wading birds.

BARTOLOMÉ ISLAND

This tiny island off the southeast coast of Santiago is one of the most photographed sights in the archipelago. A wooden staircase leads 114 meters up to a summit with a breathtaking view—and for once, this is no exaggeration. In the foreground the mangroves are flanked on either side by twin half-moon beaches. Rising up behind is the famous 40-meter Pinnacle Rock, a jagged lava formation, which has endured years of erosion as well as the U.S. Air Force using it for target practice during World War II. The blackened lava fields of Santiago in the background complete a perfect photograph.

A dry landing is followed by a 30-minute round-trip hike to take in the view. It's a steep but short climb. Afterward, you take a short boat ride to the two beaches, where there is excellent snorkeling with a small colony of sea lions as well as the occasional chance to see Galápagos penguins. Out of the water, a trail winds through the mangroves to the beach on the other side. Swimming is not allowed on this side, but look closely and you may glimpse stingrays, white-tipped sharks, and sea turtles that come ashore at night to lay their eggs. In the mangroves, bird-watchers should keep their eyes open for Galápagos hawks, herons, and oystercatchers. Bartolomé is included on many cruise itineraries, but as a day trip it has become more expensive and will set you back $125 per person with tour operators in Puerto Ayora.

RÁBIDA ISLAND

About five kilometers south of Santiago, this small island, also known as Jervis, is the exact geographic center of the Galápagos archipelago. There's a wet landing onto a rust-colored beach filled with dozens of sea lions stretched out; this is a great spot to walk among a colony and listen to their snorts and snoring. It's also an excellent place for snorkeling, but note that the male sea lion population is quite large (it's mainly a bachelor colony), so take care. The beach is also one of the best places in the archipelago to see brown pelicans nesting. Chicks have a high mortality rate, so don't be surprised to stumble across numerous corpses, but there are plenty of live ones filling the skies and crying to their parents, who are busy dive-bombing the oceans in search of the family lunch.

A 750-meter trail leads up to the island's 367-meter volcanic peak, which is covered in fragrant *palo santo* trees. There are good views

> # TRAVELS WITH CHARLIE
>
> The staple article of animal food is supplied by the tortoises. Their numbers have of course been greatly reduced on this island, but the people yet count on two days' hunting giving them food for the rest of the week. It is said that the formerly single vessels have taken away as many as seven hundred, and that the ship's company of a frigate some years since brought down in one day two hundred tortoises to the beach.
>
> Charles Darwin in *The Voyage of the Beagle*, on the marked effect of human colonization of Floreana on the giant tortoise population

over the steep cliffs on the other side. On the trail, look for Galápagos hawks perched watchfully on tree branches as well as Galápagos flamingos and yellow-crowned night herons stabbing at fish and shrimp in the salt ponds.

SOMBRERO CHINO

This tiny island off the southeast tip of Santiago, just south of Bartolomé, is a volcanic cone with the rough shape of a "Chinese hat" (hence the name). Most cruise tours simply pass it to admire the shape because landing access is restricted to boats carrying 12 people or fewer. There's a small sea lion colony, marine iguanas, excellent snorkeling, and a short 700-meter trail across the island, which takes half an hour and commands impressive views.

Western Islands

Isabela and Fernandina are the youngest islands in the archipelago with the most dramatic volcanic landscapes. They are also less visited than the central and southern islands, which only adds to their appeal.

From Isabela's port, **Puerto Villamil,** there are several visitor sites close to town, notably the **Tortoise Breeding Center** (the largest in the archipelago) and the islets of **Las Tintoreras,** which offer great snorkeling with reef sharks. In the highlands, one of the best hikes in the Galápagos is to the steaming sulfur mines of **Sierra Negra,** Isabela's highest volcano, which boasts the second-largest crater in the world. Marine sites only accessible to cruise boats include *panga* rides into the mangroves of **Punta Moreno** to see penguins and **Elizabeth Bay** to see flightless cormorants. **Urbina Bay** contains a fascinating raised coral reef, and **Tagus Cove** is notable for the graffiti left by generations of pirates as well as a hike to the deep-blue saline **Darwin Lake.**

West of Isabela is the archipelago's youngest and most volcanically active island, **Fernandina.** There is one visitor site at **Punta Espinosa,** which has a large population of nesting flightless cormorants, the largest colony of marine iguanas in the archipelago, and a large sea lion colony.

ISABELA ISLAND

Isabela is by far the largest island in the Galápagos and at nearly 4,600 square kilometers accounts for half the archipelago's total land mass. At 100 kilometers long, it's four times the size of Santa Cruz, the next largest island. The landscape is dominated by six intermittently active volcanoes. From north to south: Wolf (1,646 meters) and Ecuador (610 meters), which both straddle the equator; Darwin (1,280 meters); Alcedo (1,097 meters);

Sierra Negra (1,490 meters); and Cerro Azul (1,250 meters), which was the most recent to erupt, in May 2008.

The island's only port, Puerto Villamil, where most of the island's population of 2,000 live, is slowly turning into a tourism hub, but on a much smaller scale than Puerto Ayora and Baquerizo Moreno. There are plenty of visitor sites near the port as well as excursions inland to the volcanoes, but many of the best coastal sites are on the west side of Isabela, only accessible to cruises. Most cruises stick to the central and southern islands in the archipelago, and fewer than 25 percent make it out to Isabela due to the distance involved. Those that do are rewarded with some spectacular visitor sites.

As the giant of the archipelago, it's only fitting that Isabela has one of the largest populations of giant tortoises, which feed on the abundant vegetation in the highlands. There are five separate subspecies here, one for each volcano (except tiny Volcán Ecuador). The slopes of Volcán Alcedo have the biggest population—more than 35 percent of all the tortoises in the archipelago.

The west coast of the island receives nutrient-rich cool waters from both the Humboldt and Cromwell Currents. This is why the marine life is so abundant, with large populations of whales, dolphins, and flightless cormorants, which dive down into the cool waters in search of fish and no longer need their wings. Isabela also has the largest populations of Galápagos penguins, although numbers fell dramatically as a result of the 1998 El Niño climate pattern.

The tortoise population on Isabela has suffered considerably. The whalers used to hunt them, and more recently thousands of feral goats have eaten their vegetation; cows and donkeys trample their eggs. Volcanic eruptions and a human-caused fire that raged for five months in

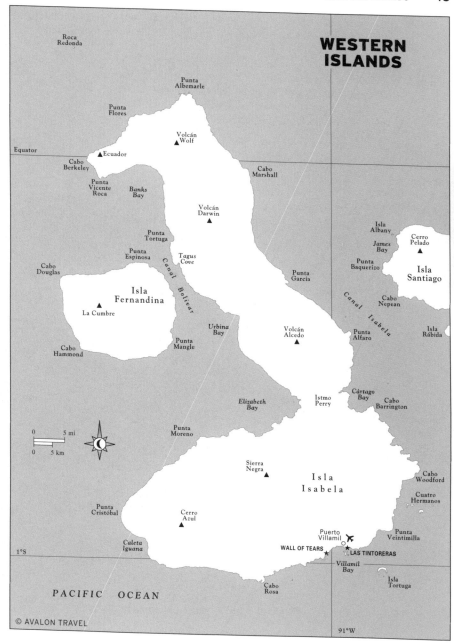

WESTERN
ISLANDS

Roca
Redonda

Punta
Albemarle

Punta
Flores

Volcán
▲Wolf

Equator

Cabo
Berkeley   ▲Ecuador

Cabo
Marshall

Punta
Vicente   Banks
Roca   Bay

Volcán
Darwin
▲

Punta
Tortuga   Isla
Punta   Tagus   Albany
Espinosa   Cove   Cerro
Cabo   James   Pelado
Douglas   Bay   ▲

Isla   Punta   Isla
Fernandina   Baquerizo Santiago
▲
La Cumbre   Punta   Cabo
                       García   Nepean
              Urbina
              Bay   Volcán   Isla
Cabo   Punta   Alcedo   Punta   Rábida
Hammond   Mangle   ▲   Alfaro

                                     Cártago
                       Istmo   Bay   Cabo
              Elizabeth Perry   Barrington
              Bay

0   5 mi   Punta
              Moreno
0   5 km
                       Sierra   Cabo
                       Negra   Isla   Woodford
                       ▲   Isabela
                                                       Cuatro
                                                       Hermanos

Punta
Cristóbal   Cerro
              Azul
              ▲
                                    Puerto   Punta
                                    Villamil   Veintimilla
       Caleta
       Iguana   WALL OF TEARS ★   LAS TINTORERAS
1°S
                                              Villamil
                                              Bay   Isla
                                                       Tortuga
PACIFIC   OCEAN   Cabo
                            Rosa
© AVALON TRAVEL   91°W

Canal Bolivar

Canal Isabela

1984 have also ravaged the landscapes. Things are improving, though, particularly after 100,000 goats were successfully eradicated in the past decade by a huge government operation, mainly employing Australian hunters in helicopters. The tortoise breeding center on the island is one of the biggest in the archipelago, releasing hundreds of tortoises back into the wild.

History

Whalers and pirates began visiting Isabela in the 18th century, hunting in the waters off the west coast and stopping over to gather tortoises as food for long voyages. The names of many of these ships are still carved into the rocks at Tagus Cove.

In 1946, it was the humans' turn to endure hardships on the island when a penal colony was built on the Sierra Negra's southern slopes. The best evidence of the brutal regime is the lava-rock Muro de las Lágrimas (Wall of Tears), which still stands near Puerto Villamil, a thoroughly pointless construction sweated over by luckless convicts over many years. Food supplies were scarce in those days, and it was usually consumed by the guards, leaving many convicts to starve to death. The notorious jail was closed in 1959.

Puerto Villamil

About 2,000 people live in this small port on the southeast tip of Isabela. As well as fishing and a developing tourism industry, the locals have worked on all manner of projects—from sulfur mining in nearby Sierra Negra volcano to lime production and coffee farming. The town is quite charming and a far more laid-back base than the two larger ports in the archipelago. With a small selection of hotels and restaurants as well as nearby beaches, a lagoon, and highland hikes, there's plenty to keep you busy for a few days.

West of Isabela, nothing but thousands of miles of Pacific Ocean stretches all the way to French Polynesia.

RECREATION AND TOURS

At the western edge of town is a set of lagoons with sizeable populations of flamingos that flock here to mate. **Poza de los Diablos** (Devil's Pool) is actually the largest lagoon in the entire archipelago. Wooden walkways take you past the lagoons before joining a trail through a forest.

Continue along the trail for 20 minutes (or take a taxi for $2) to reach the **Centro de Crianza** (Tortoise Breeding Center), a more impressive tortoise breeding center than the one found at Charles Darwin Station on Santa Cruz. There are some 850 tortoises separated into eight enclosures as well as an information center documenting the life cycle of these fascinating creatures and an excellent program to boost the populations of Isabela's five subspecies.

Continue along the coast to the west for another 30 minutes to reach the **Muro de las Lágrimas (Wall of Tears),** built by convicts from a penal colony in the 1940s. It's just a wall, but the brutal story behind it is interesting. The wall is 100 meters long and 7 meters high and served no real purpose except punishment, which only adds to the tragedy of the men who suffered and died building it. There is a set of steps up to an impressive view of the wall and the surrounding landscape. It's quite a walk to the wall—about an hour from town—so it's best done out of the heat of the day, or consider taking a taxi ($5) or a guided tour ($20 pp). You may be tempted to go swimming to cool off on the way back, and there is good surfing on the beaches west of the port.

Southeast of town is the best spot for snorkeling, a set of islets called **Las Tintoreras,** named after the reef sharks that frequent them. You can also spot sea lions, turtles, penguins, and white-tipped sharks resting in the canals or under rocks. There is also a short trail around the islets, where sally lightfoot crabs scuttle. The islets are reachable from a jetty, but you must be accompanied by a guide. A tour costs $25 per person and lasts 1-2 hours.

There are a couple of tour operators on the main plaza. The best is **Nautilus** (Gil and Las Fragatas, tel. 5/252-9076, www.nautilustour. com). Tours to the Wall of Tears and various sites west of town cost $20 per person, snorkeling at Las Tintoreras costs $20 per person, and hikes to Sierra Negra cost from $40 per person, depending on the group size.

ACCOMMODATIONS

There are fewer hotels in Puerto Villamil than in Baquerizo Moreno and Puerto Ayora, but prices are lower, and because the port is relatively quiet, it's possible to negotiate because hotels don't fill up that often. Accommodations on the beach are slightly pricier than inland. The best option for those on a tight budget is the informal **Posada del Caminante** (near Cormorán, tel. 5/252-9407, $15 s, $20 d), a 15-minute walk inland. Most guest rooms have kitchens, and there's a communal fridge and free laundry. In the center of town, the best value budget hotels are **Rincón de George** (16 de Marzo and Gil, tel. 5/252-9214, $20 s, $30 d) and **Hostal Villamil** (16 de Marzo and Gil, tel. 5/252-9180, $20 s, $30 d) next door. Both offer comfortably furnished guest rooms with firm beds, hot water, and air-conditioning. The owner of Rincón de George is a registered tour guide. On the beach, you can find great ocean views and decent guest rooms at **The Dolphin House** (Gil, tel. 5/252-9138, $30 s, $45 d, breakfast included), but beware of the pair of cockerels that are guaranteed to wake you up before dawn. Opposite is another attractive mid-range choice, **Volcano Hotel** (Gil, tel. 5/252-9034, $25 s, $40 d) with colorful guest rooms that have recently been renovated.

A few blocks inland, popular with tour groups, a mid-range option is **San Vicente** (Cormorán and Las Escalecias, tel. 5/252-9140, $30 s, $60 d, breakfast included), with

THE GALÁPAGOS ISLANDS

comfortable guest rooms, private baths, air-conditioning, and hot water.

Puerto Villamil is beginning to cater to luxury land-based tours, and some top-end hotels have opened in the past few years. The swankiest hotel on the beach is the ideally located British-run **Albemarle** (Gil, tel. 5/252-9489, www.hotelalbemarle.com, $150 s or d, breakfast included). This two-story Mediterranean-style villa has guest rooms with stylish stone baths, high ceilings, and all the amenities. At the east end of town, the homely **Casa Marita** (Gil, tel. 5/252-9301, www.casamaritagalapagos.com, $65 s, $100 d) has uniquely decorated guest rooms and suites. There's a jetted tub, a bar, a restaurant, and hammocks in the garden. Farther along, walking out of town toward the tortoise breeding center, is the newest top-end hotel, **Iguana Crossing** (Gil, tel. 5/252-9484, www.iguanacrossing.com.ec, $200 s or d), with immaculate guest rooms, a beautiful pool facing the beach, a spa, and a gourmet restaurant.

FOOD

Restaurant options in Puerto Villamil are rather limited, mostly concentrated along the main road, Antonio Gil, which runs parallel to the beach. Most restaurants do set menus for $4, although you often have to ask for it as they prefer to push the pricier menu items. The best restaurant in the center is probably **La Choza** (Gil, no phone, lunch and dinner daily, entrées $8-15), which serves hearty portions of barbecued meats in a rustic thatched hut. Farther along, **El Encanto de la Pepa** (Gil, no phone, lunch and dinner daily, entrées $5-7) is another good option, particularly for ceviche, breaded shrimp, and grilled fish. A cheaper option is **Tres Hermanos** (Gil, no phone, breakfast, lunch, and dinner daily, entrées $3-6), which offers set meals, snacks, and burgers.

After dinner, there is very little nightlife, but a good place for a drink is **Bar Beto** (Gil, no phone, 7 P.M.-midnight Mon.-Sat.), a beach bar at the western edge of town. The cocktails are rather pricey, but the beer goes down well with the sea view.

INFORMATION AND SERVICES

The local iTur tourist office (16 de Marzo and Las Fragatas, tel. 5/301-6648) is two blocks inland. The **National Park office** (Gil and Piqueros, tel. 5/252-9178) is one block from the main plaza.

Note that there is no bank or ATM on Isabela; some top-end hotels accept credit cards, but you are strongly advised to bring enough cash for the duration of your stay.

GETTING THERE AND AROUND

Buses leave daily for the highlands, but you're better off exploring on a guided tour. **Taxis** can be picked up from near the main plaza and will take you around town for $1 and to nearby visitor sites for a little more. **Emetebe** (Gil, tel. 5/252-9255) has flights to San Cristóbal and Baltra ($160 pp one-way). *Lanchas* (speed-boat ferries) shuttle to Puerto Ayora (2.5 hours, $30 pp one-way) daily at 6 A.M. from the main dock.

Sierra Negra and the Highlands

The best excursion to take from Puerto Villamil, and perhaps the most impressive geological sight in the entire archipelago, is the hike up to the active Sierra Negra, Isabela's oldest and highest volcano. The last eruption was in 2005 and took geologists by surprise, so you can't trek right to the crater. However, there are two excellent treks—the shorter is to **Volcán Chico,** a fissure of lava cones northwest of the main crater. On this side, there is less mist and rain, offering spectacular views over the north of Isabela and across to Fernandina. This trek takes about four hours and is usually a combination of hiking and horseback riding. The longer trek is to **Las Minas de Azufre** (Sulfur Mines).

© BEN WESTWOOD

Sierra Negra has the second-largest volcanic crater in the world.

It takes about six or seven hours in total and is tougher, particularly in the rainy season, when it gets very muddy. However, your toils will be rewarded with fantastic views of the crater, which at 10 kilometers in diameter is the second largest in the world after Ngorongoro in Tanzania. The hike culminates in a dramatic descent into the yellow hills of the sulfur mines, which spew out choking gas (hold your breath!). Both treks can be booked with the tour operators in the port, but note that the longer trek is less common, so booking ahead is essential. **Nautilus** (Gil and Las Fragatas, tel. 5/252-9076, www.nautilustour.com) charges $40 per person. Wilmer Quezada (tel. 8/687-8626 or 5/252-9326) is a particularly good local guide.

Marine Sites

All of the following visitor sites are off-limits to land-based visitors and are only accessible to cruise tours.

PUNTA MORENO

This visitor site is often the first point on Isabela for boats approaching from the south. It is reachable via a *panga* ride along the sea cliffs and into a grove of mangroves where penguins and great blue herons are often seen. After a dry landing, a two-kilometer hike inland along a *pahoehoe* lava flow lined by cacti leads to a handful of brackish ponds frequented in season by flamingos and white-cheeked pintail. There are impressive views of three of Isabela's volcanoes. Wear comfortable shoes because the lava rocks are difficult to negotiate in places, and note that it's quite a strenuous hike, so take plenty of water and sunblock.

ELIZABETH BAY

North of Punta Moreno, Elizabeth Bay has no landing site, so it can only be explored by *panga*. There are small populations of flightless cormorants and marine iguanas in the bay. The marine iguanas here are comparatively big, munching themselves to a healthy size on the abundant supplies of algae. Farther in is a set of shallow lagoons where you can see rays, turtles, and occasionally white-tipped sharks. The *panga* then heads out to some rocky islets called Las Marielas, where there is a small colony of nesting penguins.

URBINA BAY

This bay was created by remarkable geological activity in 1954. A volcanic eruption lifted a chunk of seabed, including a coral reef, six meters above the water's surface. After a wet landing on the beach, you can enjoy the somewhat surreal experience of seeing coral littered with bones and the shells of marine life. The short loop trail takes less than two hours. Flightless cormorants and pelicans nest here, marine iguanas can be seen, and there are rays and sea turtles in the bay.

TAGUS COVE

Tagus Cove is the best place to see how humans have left their mark—literally—on the Galápagos Islands. The rocks above this popular anchorage in the Bolívar Channel are covered in graffiti. It's a strange but interesting sight, with the oldest readable record from whalers dating from 1836.

The two-kilometer hike from the cove to the interior is quite strenuous but worth the effort. A dry landing leads to a trail through a steep gully to a wooden staircase and then along a gravel track. At the top is an impressive view over the deep blue **Darwin Lake.** This eroded crater is 12 meters deep, and the waters have a high salt content, so it's largely lifeless. Scientists have concluded that seawater seeped in through the porous lava rocks beneath the surface. The small round pebbles covering the trails began as raindrops that collected airborne volcanic ash and hardened before hitting the ground. The trail leads to the lower lava slopes of Darwin Volcano, and

there are spectacular views over the entire island of Isabela.

After the hike, there is a *panga* ride, and you can cool off with some good snorkeling along the rocky northern shore. Highlights include sea turtles, Galápagos penguins, flightless cormorants, and sea lions.

OTHER SITES

There are various other sites on Isabela, most of which have restricted access. Just north of Tagus Cove is **Punta Tortuga,** a beach surrounded by mangroves, and one of the few spots to see the mangrove finch. Farther north, **Punta Vicente Roca** has good snorkeling and diving but no landing site at the base of small Volcán Ecuador. At Isabela's northern tip, **Punta Albemarle** was a U.S. radar base in World War II. There is no landing site, but there is plenty of birdlife to see from the boat, including flightless cormorants and penguins.

On the east side of Isabela, there is a landing site at **Punta García,** one of the few places on this side where flightless cormorants can be seen. This is the beginning for the trail up to **Volcán Alcedo,** famous for its seven-kilometer-wide crater. The 14-kilometer ascent takes 6-7 hours. Along the way is a fascinating landscape of steaming fumaroles, ancient craters, lava flows, abundant birdlife, and hundreds of giant tortoises living on the volcano's slopes. Special permits must be obtained for this hike, which involves a time-consuming bureaucratic process, and it's not included on most itineraries.

FERNANDINA ISLAND

Fernandina is special even by Galápagos standards. The westernmost island in the archipelago is one of the few that has escaped invasion by introduced species, and the island's pristine ecosystem has been preserved. This island is also less visited than most of the others due to its remote location, and it retains the air of a land that time forgot.

At under one million years old, Fernandina is the youngest volcanic island in the archipelago and also the most active. The volcano, La Cumbre, has erupted several times in recent years, most spectacularly in 1968 when the caldera collapsed more than 300 meters, and most recently in April 2009.

Punta Espinosa

Fernandina has just one visitor site, Punta Espinosa, on the island's northeast corner across from Isabela's Tagus Cove, but it's arguably one of the best sites in the archipelago. A dry landing among the mangroves leads 250 meters to a sandy point partly covered by rough lava from recent flows. Nearby is the dramatic sight of the largest colony of marine iguanas in the archipelago sunning themselves on the rocks. Look carefully and you can spot their nests in the sand.

Next you pass a large sea lion colony with the sound of barking bulls filling the air. This is also one of the biggest nesting sites of flightless cormorants. Watch out for males returning from fishing to bring lunch to their mate, who sits in a tangled nest of seaweed and twigs near the water's edge.

After retracing your steps, there is a longer 750-meter trail leading over jagged lava spotted with lava cacti (bring good shoes). Brilliant vermillion flycatchers often sit in the mangrove branches. At low tide there is a pool that offers excellent bird-watching. The tour usually ends with a *panga* ride out into the strait, where schools of dolphins are often seen. There is excellent snorkeling at several locations around Punta Espinosa, offering chances to see penguins, marine iguanas, flightless cormorants, and sea turtles.

THE GALÁPAGOS ISLANDS

Southern Islands

South of Santa Cruz, Floreana can be visited both on day trips and on cruises. The island has a fascinating history, beautiful landscapes in the highlands, a rather quirky post office, and excellent snorkeling. Española is no longer reachable on day trips, so you need to be on a cruise tour to see the albatross.

Floreana's best sites include **Punta Cormorant,** which has populations of flamingos and other wading birds; the centuries-old post box at **Post Office Bay;** and excellent snorkeling spots at the submerged volcanic cone of **Devil's Crown,** along with **Enderby** and **Champion Island.**

On Española's west side, **Punta Suárez** is not to be missed—it's the biggest breeding site in the world for waved albatross and a great place to see them taking off, landing, and performing their dancing mating ritual. On the northeast side of the island there are

opportunities to snorkel with sea lions, reef sharks, and marine turtles at **Gardner Bay.**

FLOREANA ISLAND

As the lush hills of Floreana come into view, it's difficult to believe that such a serene island could have such a troubled history. The population of the island today stands at less than 200, but Floreana was actually the first island in the archipelago to be populated.

History

In the 18th century, whalers and pirates were drawn to a rare spring water supply in the hills as well as fresh meat in the form of the island's giant tortoises. Rats, cats, and goats were introduced to Floreana, causing untold damage and decimating the tortoise population. The whalers would spend so long at sea that they decided to set up a post office on the island as the only

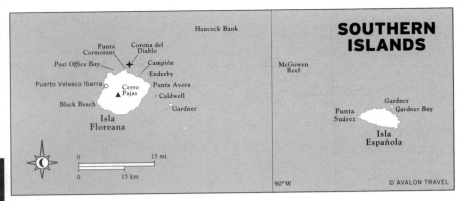

means of communicating with their families. You can still see evidence of the early settlers in carvings in the rocks of caves in the highlands.

In 1807, Floreana had its first permanent resident, Irishman Patrick Watkins. He was marooned here and lived for two years by growing vegetables. Eventually, he stole a ship's longboat, took a small crew, but arrived alone in Guayaquil weeks later. Nobody knows what became of his crew.

After Ecuador's independence in 1830, Floreana was named after the country's first president, Juan José Flores, and it became a penal colony. Soon afterward in 1841 Herman Melville, author of *Moby Dick,* visited the island and wrote about its history, increasing worldwide interest.

In the 1930s, the arrival of several German settlers looking for an escape to paradise further disturbed Floreana's tiny community. First a reclusive dentist, Dr. Friedrich Ritter, arrived with his lover, followed by the Wittmer family; finally, a troublesome woman who claimed to be a baroness arrived with three lovers. The story of death and disappearance that ensued is a tale worthy of a Hollywood movie and has been recounted in several books.

Nowadays, Floreana is a comparatively quiet island. While the archipelago's three other ports have developed apace, Puerto Velasco

Ibarra has a population of less than 200. Of the invasive species, goats have been eradicated, but rats are far more difficult to remove, and the endemic mockingbird is just one species that is now endangered as a result. The tortoise population, which was hunted to extinction on Floreana in the 19th century, has been boosted by a breeding center in the highlands. There are day trips to Floreana daily from Santa Cruz; very few visitors stay on the island, although there are a couple of hotels.

Puerto Velasco Ibarra

This tiny port lives in comparative isolation from the rest of the islands. There are few basic services, which is why most visits are confined to day trips. There are no banks, electricity is restricted, and the only mail service is through the Post Office Bay barrel.

There are a couple of hotels on the island, and it's possible that in the next decade Floreana may develop further, but it's anybody's guess. The **Pensión Wittmer** (tel. 5/252-0150 or 5/252-9506, $30 s, $50 d) has guest rooms and bungalows overlooking the beach with fans, private baths, and hot water. Three meals cost an additional $20 per person. **Red Mangrove Lava Lodge** (tel. 5/252-4905 on Floreana, 5/252-6564 on Santa Cruz, www.redmangrove.com, $168 s, $186 d, breakfast

© BEN WESTWOOD

Floreana Island has spectacular landscapes, but a troubled history.

included) has been built recently—10 ocean-front pine cabins sleep 2-3 with private baths and porches overlooking a black lava beach.

Buses leave for the highlands early every morning. It's a 30-minute drive or a three-hour walk eight kilometers into the highlands to the **Asilo de la Paz,** the island's only water source. If you decide to stay on the island, you can sometimes hitch a ride back to Puerto Ayora with one of the day tours.

Punta Cormorant

Visiting this site on the north side of Floreana starts with a wet landing onto a beach colored green by olivine minerals, which are silicates of magnesium and iron. A 720-meter trail leads up to a saltwater lagoon. Along the trail, Floreana's comparatively lush surroundings can be appreciated. The lagoon is a good spot to see flamingos and other wading birds such as white-cheeked pintail, stilt, and gallinules. The lagoon is surrounded by gray, seemingly lifeless *palo santo* trees. Among the vegetation is abundant birdlife, including yellow warblers and flycatchers. Beyond is a beautiful beach, nicknamed "flour beach" for its incredibly fine white sand. Stingrays and spotted eagle rays are common near the beach, and sea turtles nest here November-February. There are signs to keep out of their nesting areas, but you may be lucky enough to see them swimming. Note that snorkeling and swimming here are not allowed. The only drawback of this site is its perplexing name—there are no flightless cormorants here.

Post Office Bay

Post Office Bay is one of the quirkiest sites in the Galápagos. You wouldn't imagine that a mailbox would be of much appeal, but it has an interesting history and is also a bit of light-hearted fun. Back in 1793, whalers began the practice of leaving mail in a barrel for home-ward-bound ships to collect. Crews would then hand-deliver the letters to their destination in a remarkable act of camaraderie. These days the tradition has been carried on, mainly by tourists. Leave a postcard for a fellow national to collect, and take one home with you. Tradition dictates that you should deliver it in person, but paying the postage is probably preferable these days to turning up on a stranger's doorstep. The barrel has evolved into a wooden box on a pole surrounded by an assortment of junk.

A visit to the bay begins with a wet landing directly onto the brown-sand beach. Just a few meters beyond the barrel is a lava tunnel, and you often need to wade through water to reach it. There are also the rusted remains of a Norwegian fish operation dating back to the 1920s as well as a football field used by crews who may invite you to a game. Be aware that there are sizeable populations of introduced wasps, and their sting is painful, so take care. A more scenic end to the visit is a *panga* ride past a sea lion colony, where you can also spot sea turtles and occasionally penguins.

Devil's Crown

Offshore from Post Office Bay, the jagged peaks of this submerged volcanic cone poke out of the water and supply its name, Corona del Diablo (Devil's Crown). The nooks and crannies of this marine site offer some of the best snorkeling in the islands, either outside the ring or in the shallow inner chamber, which is reached through a side opening. There is a rich variety of tropical fish—parrot fish, angelfish, and damselfish—and you can occasionally see sea lions and sharks. Note that the current can be quite strong on the seaward side, so pay close attention to your guide.

Enderby and Champion Island

These two sites are very popular with snorkelers and divers. Enderby is an eroded tuff cone where you can snorkel with playful sea lions, and Champion Island is a small offshore crater,

a popular nesting site for boobies. Landing is not allowed, but the snorkeling is good.

La Lobería

If you come on a day tour, after visiting the port and the interior of the island, this is the main site. There is a 900-meter path on the beach, but day tours are limited to snorkeling offshore. There is a small population of sea lions as well as marine turtles.

ESPAÑOLA ISLAND

The southernmost island in the Galápagos is also the oldest in the archipelago, at nearly 3.5 million years, compared with Fernandina in the northwest, which is less than one million years old. The island's reputation as one of the top spots for bird-watching has led to the phasing-out of day trips from San Cristóbal and Santa Cruz, and you need to be on a cruise to come here now. The waved albatross that nest here April-November are the island's main draw. Witness these enormous birds taking off and landing, and enjoy their amusing mating dance.

Gardner Bay

On the northeast side of Española, this beautiful crescent beach is reached by a wet landing. There are no hikes, so the main draw is the excellent snorkeling. Highlights include frolicking with playful sea lions (there's a colony here) as well as spotting stingrays or occasional white-tipped sharks. The beach is an important nesting site for marine turtles, so you might be lucky enough to see them. **Turtle Rock,** a short *panga* ride offshore, is another good snorkeling spot with a rich variety of bright tropical fish such as moorish idols, damselfish, and parrot fish.

On the beach, you can walk among the sea lion colony, although try to give the males a wide berth. At the east end, there are marine iguanas and sally lightfoot crabs, and you can often see the endemic hood mockingbirds.

Punta Suárez

On the west tip of Española, Punta Suárez is one of the top visitor sites in the Galápagos. A wet landing leads to a trail toward the cliffs on the south side of the point. Along the way, there is a large blue-footed booby colony; watch your step, as these tame birds remain utterly unconcerned by your presence and sit in the middle of the trail.

The best is yet to come. If you visit between April and November, farther along the trail is the biggest breeding site of waved albatross in the world, and this site is even nicknamed "albatross airport." Some 15,000 couples congregate on the island, and it's quite a sight to witness these massive birds with their 2.5-meter wing spans taking off from the cliffs. Seeing them land is also impressive

but rather less elegant, as they often fall over, being unsteady on their feet after long flights. The highlight is their entertaining courtship, as the couple dance around each other in a synchronized circular walk, clacking and calling skyward.

This site is teeming with birdlife, and aside from the boobies and albatross, you can see Galápagos hawks, Galápagos doves, swallow-tailed gulls, oystercatchers, red-billed tropic birds, and finches. The views of the cliffs below are equally impressive, with waves crashing into rocks and water spurting high into the air through blowholes. The rocks are often covered in marine iguanas sunning themselves; these iguanas are more colorful than those found on other islands, with turquoise tinges to their backs and legs, perhaps the result of eating algae endemic to Española.

The entire trail is about 1,600 meters and takes about two hours.

Northern Islands

Genovesa, Darwin, and Wolf are the most remote islands that can be visited in the archipelago, and most boats need to travel overnight. Each has its unique attractions: Genovesa for its birds, particularly red-footed boobies at **Darwin Bay Beach** and **Prince Philip's Steps**; and Darwin and Wolf rank among the best dive sites in the world.

GENOVESA

Genovesa, also known as Tower Island or even Booby Island, is famed for its abundant birdlife, notably red-footed boobies, but it takes some getting to—about eight hours by boat overnight, so stock up on seasickness tablets. Interestingly, there are no land reptiles on Genovesa, only a small population of marine iguanas.

Darwin Bay Beach

After a tricky entrance into the bay, where you pass rocks decorated with graffiti from visiting ships, there is a wet landing onto the beach. A 1.5-kilometer trail leads inland to the salt-bushes filled with the nests of red-footed boobies and frigate birds. Masked boobies and swallow-tailed gulls also nest here, and you may spot storm petrels and short-eared owls.

Another branch of the trail leads over rough rocks next to a series of tidal pools, where you can see yellow-crowned night herons half-asleep by day. Other species to watch for include mockingbirds, Galápagos doves, and Darwin's finches. The opuntia cacti you see on the trail are noticeably softer than on other islands. Scientists believe this is because the plants don't need to defend themselves against

THE GALÁPAGOS ISLANDS

giant tortoises (there has never been a tortoise population on the island).

Prince Philip's Steps

Named in honor of a royal visit in the 1960s and also known as El Barranco, this site near the tip of Darwin Bay's eastern arm is limited to boats of 16 people or fewer. A *panga* ride along the bottom of the cliffs provides glimpses of red-billed tropic birds landing in their crevice nests and a large population of frigate birds. If you're lucky, you may glimpse elusive fur seals. Ashore, a steep-railed stairway leads to a dramatic 1.5-kilometer trail along the top of the cliffs. Masked and red-footed boobies nest here with frigate birds lurking nearby, ready to scavenge. It's also a good area to see Galápagos doves and sharp-beaked ground finches, also known as "vampire finches" because they peck away at booby's tails. Storm petrels are also seen in large numbers. The *panga* ride and hike combined take about two hours.

WOLF AND DARWIN ISLANDS

These tiny islands, about 215 kilometers northwest of the main island group, are hidden jewels visited only by diving tours. It takes a full night to get here, but the rewards are rich indeed—these islands rank among the best dives in the world. The waters around Wolf and Darwin attract whale sharks June-November. Other shark species commonly seen are hammerheads, Galápagos sharks, and reef sharks. Manta rays, dolphins, and turtles abound.

MARCHENA AND PINTA ISLANDS

Midway between Wolf and Genovesa in the far north of the archipelago, these two medium-size islands are closed to visitors, although diving is possible in the waters off the coast of Marchena. Pinta is famous as the original home of Lonesome George, and giant tortoises are currently being repopulated on the island. Marchena has a 343-meter volcano at its center that last erupted in 1991.

BACKGROUND

The Land

The Galápagos's landscapes are as diverse and otherworldly as the wildlife that inhabit them: lush highland forests, pristine white-sand beaches, steaming volcanic peaks, and blackened lava trails strewn with cacti. The 13 volcanic islands and 16 tiny islets scattered over 60,000 square kilometers in the eastern Pacific Ocean have 8,000 square kilometers of land, including 1,350 kilometers of coastline. The islands are actually the tips of underwater volcanoes, which become younger and higher to the west. Isabela, the largest island of the group at 4,275 square kilometers, has six volcanic peaks, and one of these, Cerro Azul, is the highest point on the islands at 1,689 meters.

Some 97 percent of the land mass is in the national park and uninhabited, and only the remaining 3 percent is inhabited. The latest estimated population of the archipelago is 27,000, of whom 7,000 are temporary residents. The biggest population area is Puerto Ayora on Santa Cruz, followed by the capital, Puerto Baquerizo Moreno, on San Cristóbal, then Puerto Villamil on Isabela, and tiny Puerto Velasco Ibarra on Floreana.

© MICHAEL ZYSMAN/123RF

© BEN WESTWOOD

the Sierra Negra volcano on Isabela

GEOGRAPHY
Volcanic Origins

The Galápagos sits directly over a hot spot in the Pacific tectonic plate, where underlying magma bulges closer to the surface than usual. Millions of years ago, molten rock began to rise through the crust, cooling in the sea and forming mountains that eventually rose above the surface. New volcanoes quickly formed to take the place of older ones and were slowly eroded by the sea and weather, resulting in a rough chain of islands trailing off southeast toward the mainland. Many volcanoes came and went over millions of years; Española, the oldest island in the archipelago, is nearly 3.5 million years old. By comparison Fernandina is less than one million years old, a mere infant in geological terms. Geologists have found an island forming west of Fernandina, although it will be many thousands of years or so before it forms, so don't expect it to be included on your itinerary just yet.

Evidence of volcanic heritage is everywhere on the islands. There are many lava flows that have hardened into rocky trails, the most accessible being in Sullivan Bay on Santiago. In the highlands on Santa Cruz you can find collapsed calderas and lava tunnels, while Isabela offers the best close-up view of an active volcano, with trails leading past the second-largest crater in the world at Sierra Negra and into its pungent sulfur mines. Nearby Cerro Azul erupted in May 2008. Fernandina also has trails through lava fields, and it experienced the most recent eruption at La Cumbre in April 2009.

The Sea

The islands' unique ecosystem has been created by the interaction of several ocean currents. The most famous and most powerful is the Humboldt Current, which brings cold water from the south along the coast of Chile and Peru. The warmer Panama Current flows down from Central America, and every few years it

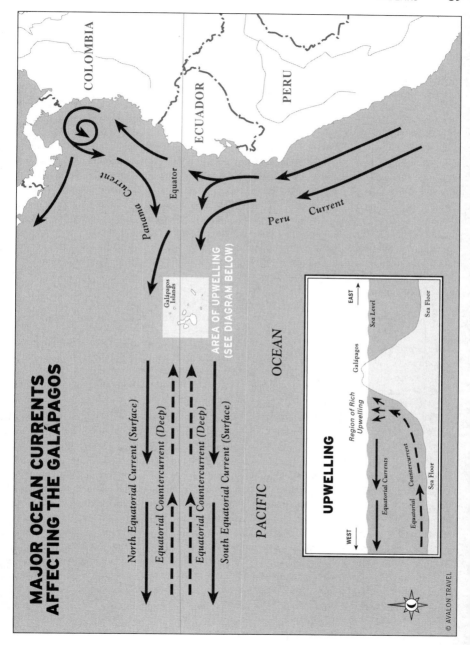

MAJOR OCEAN CURRENTS AFFECTING THE GALÁPAGOS

COLOMBIA

ECUADOR

PERU

Equator

Panama Current

Peru Current

Galápagos Islands

AREA OF UPWELLING (SEE DIAGRAM BELOW)

PACIFIC OCEAN

North Equatorial Current (Surface)

Equatorial Countercurrent (Deep)

Equatorial Countercurrent (Deep)

South Equatorial Current (Surface)

UPWELLING

WEST

EAST

Sea Level

Sea Floor

Galápagos

Region of Rich Upwelling

Equatorial Currents

Equatorial Countercurrent

Sea Floor

Sea Floor

© AVALON TRAVEL

brings devastating warm El Niño conditions, most recently in 1998. A third current is the Equatorial Counter Current (also called the Cromwell Current), which flows deep below the surface and is deflected upward when it encounters the islands, bringing cool water, which is vital to the archipelago's ecosystem. Algae thrive on the nutrients; fish and marine invertebrates feed off the algae; and whales, dolphins, sea lions, and birds eat these fish. The unusually cool waters found around the Galápagos ensure the survival of many species usually only found in colder waters, in particular the Galápagos penguins.

CLIMATE

The ocean currents described above determine the archipelago's subtropical climate. While there is no variation in hours of sunlight due to the fact that the islands are right on the equator, the temperature, cloud cover, and rainfall vary considerably throughout the year.

The hot or **rainy season** begins in December when the Panama Current warms the nearby waters to 26°C and runs until May. Daily showers bring 6-10 centimeters of precipitation per month, with more rain falling in the highlands of the larger islands. As on the coast of Ecuador, the rainy season is also the warmest period, with hot sunny days punctuated by intermittent showers. The average temperature climbs into the 30s, and the seas are comfortably warm for swimming; February and March are the warmest and sunniest months.

The June-November **dry season** arrives with the colder (20°C) waters from the Humboldt Current, and the average temperatures drop to less than 27°C. There is very little rain, but you often find *garúa,* a type of misty drizzle, in the highlands in August. Days are generally overcast, the seas colder and rougher, and the landscapes lose their greenery August-November, to be replenished again in the next rainy season. It's surprising how different the climate seems

when climbing 500 meters into the highlands-it's often quite hot and sunny on the beaches and drizzling and chilly up in the hills, so it's a good idea to bring a rain jacket and sweater when heading up there. On the larger islands of Fernandina, Isabela, Santa Cruz, and San Cristóbal, there is a distinctive type of cloud forest with mosses, lichens, and grasslands.

The biggest climatic problem in the archipelago is a lack of freshwater. The comparative lack of rain and volcanic landscapes mean that there are few sources of water in the islands. Annual rainfall in the lower elevations is a mere 6 to 10 centimeters. This is the reason why lizards, which require comparatively little water, thrive and mammals do not. For humans, this has presented serious problems. The first islands to be populated were Floreana, which has freshwater springs, and San Cristóbal, which has freshwater lakes in the highlands. On Isabela most water is extracted from wells, and on Santa Cruz it comes from brackish water (a mixture of rainwater and seawater) from *grietas,* fissures in the lava rocks. However, large quantities of drinking water have to be brought to the islands.

El Niño

It seems ironic that such a destructive climatic phenomenon should be named after the Christ child. The "devil's current" might be more appropriate, but its arrival around Christmastime gave birth to the name "the child." The phenomenon brings a surge of warm water down from the north, forcing the Humboldt Current south for up to 18 months. Ocean temperatures rise, clouds gather, and 6-10 centimeters more rain falls per month. For humans, the main problems are flooding and crop loss, but for the wildlife of the Galápagos it is even more devastating. Strong El Niño conditions struck in 1982-1983 and again in 1997-1998, and the warmer sea temperatures killed algae and fish, the main food sources for much of the wildlife.

Populations of marine iguanas, sea lions, waved albatross, penguins, and boobies fell sharply, and many still have not recovered. If past history is any indicator, a strong El Niño strikes roughly every 15 years, so the next one may be coming soon.

Environmental Issues

The Galápagos is as delicate as it is unique. In an ecological Eden with few natural predators, the arrival of one particular predator—humans—has upset the balance considerably. Only time will tell if the balance can be restored. The following is a profile of the most serious problems and what is being done to solve them.

ILLEGAL FISHING

The growth of tourism has provided a relatively easy solution to the problem of illegal fishing—people working in fishing have been persuaded that they can make more money from tourism. Many have been given assistance to set up lucrative sportfishing tours, where they catch a handful of fish daily, as opposed to box-loads. However, environmentalists claim that even sportfishing is damaging.

Illegal fishing remains a serious problem, however; fishing for lucrative sea cucumbers only stopped because the species was fished to near extinction, but shark fishing continues to be a challenge. Satellite technology has been introduced by the Ecuadorian navy, and more illegal vessels are being caught, but resources are limited. Many fishing boats use longlines that catch anything and everything, including sharks, dolphins, turtles, and seabirds. In July 2011 southeast of Genovesa, 357 dead sharks were found aboard a fishing vessel. Whether criminal proceedings will be vigorous enough to deter other poachers remains to be seen.

FOSSIL FUELS AND TRAFFIC

As tourism grows, the islands require more electricity. Historically this has come from diesel with its associated problem of causing air pollution. There are ambitious plans to convert the islands to 100 percent renewable energy by 2017, and San Cristóbal already receives more than half its energy from this scheme.

Traffic is another pressing issue. Ecuadorians love their cars, and Puerto Ayora, the archipelago's main port, is overflowing with traffic. The government has brought in measures to try to restrict car use and is proposing a new public transportation system. But there are still more than 2,000 vehicles, including 200 taxis, plying the roads of the three populated islands, bringing danger and contamination with them. All too common are road kills, not just of birds but of iguanas and other lizards, and there are even road signs warning drivers to watch for giant tortoises crossing. It makes a good photo op, but it's sad that it is necessary.

WATER POLLUTION

With rising population comes rising levels of waste, and the most pressing issue in Puerto Ayora at present is the sewage system. Freshwater has always been a problem in the archipelago, and most of Santa Cruz's freshwater comes from *grietas,* fissures in the lava rocks. The island has no adequate water treatment system, so sewage gets pumped back underground, ending up in the same reservoirs from which the town draws its water supply. Recent testing has shown that much of the island's water poses a health risk, and large areas around Puerto Ayora are polluted. Academy Bay in Santa Cruz is particularly polluted, as are some of the beaches surrounding Baquerizo Moreno on San Cristóbal. Incidents of gastritis

Road signs on the Galápagos warn drivers to watch out for iguanas, birds, tortoises, and other wildlife. Sadly, iguanas and birds are frequently killed by cars.

and food poisoning, caused by dirty water, are common. There are plans for a water treatment plant, but work is hampered by the enormous cost of drilling into the volcanic rock to construct a network of pipes. At present, the Finch Bay Eco Hotel is the only hotel that has its own water supply and sewage treatment plant.

Another problem that affects the marine ecosystem is pollution from marine fuel. With increasing numbers of vessels in the archipelago, diesel is particularly harmful to the coral. To cut costs, many boats use the cheapest fuel available, but the government is bringing in regulations to increase the use of less damaging biofuels.

INTRODUCED SPECIES

While humans have long posed a threat to the fragile ecosystem of the Galápagos, the animals and plants that they have brought with them have caused the most serious problems. There

are believed to be nearly 1,000 introduced species in the archipelago. The vast majority are plants and insects, and fruit flies and fire ants have proven to be very difficult to remove. Larger creatures that have been introduced include 12 species of mammals, 6 species of birds, and 4 species of reptiles.

Introduced Animals

Most of the introduced mammals were brought over as domestic animals—either livestock, beasts of burden, or pets—before escaping into the wild. They all cause damage in their own way. **Donkeys** eat through cactus-tree trunks to get at the juicy pulp, killing the plant in the process. Scattered **horses** and **cattle** roam the highlands, trampling on tortoise eggs, and the feral **pigs** are the worst enemy of giant tortoises, gobbling up as many turtle eggs as they can find and sometimes killing hatchlings.

Wild **dogs** are even more bloodthirsty.

While pigs kill only for food, wild dogs have been responsible for senseless attacks on iguanas, sea lions, seals, and birds, particularly on Santa Cruz. **Cats** adapt very easily to the wild and are the biggest threat to small birds and chicks on many islands.

While these large animals have wreaked havoc, they are at least relatively easy to spot. **Rats,** on the other hand, have been on the Galápagos even longer, arriving on whaling ships. As any city sanitation worker will tell you, they are extremely difficult to control. Black rats and Norway rats are the most common species. They spread disease to other species and are as much a danger as pigs to giant tortoises, eating hatchlings. In the past year the national park has been trialing poison pellets to eliminate rats from smaller islands such as Rábida, Bartolomé, and Plaza. It has been an effective program so far, but the problem is that the pellets are dangerous to Galápagos hawks, so the birds must be removed from the islands during the extermination process. Applying this method to the larger islands is fraught with difficulties.

Of all the introduced animals, the most damage has arguably been done by **goats.** They eat their way through pretty much anything, demolishing island vegetation and causing both erosion and food shortages for endemic species. They also reproduce at an astonishing rate—three goats left on Pinta in the late 1950s had produced more than 40,000 descendants by 1970. Luckily, goats are also very easy to eliminate, and some 250,000 have been culled in a large-scale extermination program on Isabela, Floreana, and Santiago. At present, only San Cristóbal, Santa Cruz, and the populated southern part of Isabela have remnant goat populations, but most are in enclosed areas.

Amphibians were the only one of five classes of vertebrates that hadn't colonized the Galápagos—until 1998, that is, when a small species of **tree frog** was first captured on Isabela and Santa Cruz. Scientists think the frogs arrived in cargo ships and were able to establish sustainable breeding populations during the particularly wet 1997-1998 El Niño conditions.

Insects have caused major problems too, the worst offenders being fire ants. These highly aggressive ants invade birds' nests as well as iguana and tortoise eggs. However, progress is being made to combat them. On the remote island of Marchena, insecticide has been trialed successfully to eliminate them, and the program will be extended to other islands, but it's a very slow process and will take many years. It also remains to be seen if the insecticide can be used over larger areas without degrading the ecosystem.

Introduced Plants

The growing human population has brought enormous numbers of plants to the archipelago—more than 500 species is the latest estimate, and most of these have arrived in the past few decades. As any gardener can confirm, unwanted plants can strangle the life out of the endemic species, stealing sun, water, and nutrients. The main offenders are fruits—vines such as passion fruit (*maracuyá*) and blackberry (*mora*) grow quickly into impenetrable thickets, and trees such as the guava and red quinine take over entire hillsides. Weeds and flowers have spread from gardens to formerly arid zones on the major islands. Of all the plants, guava trees are perhaps the worst threat, and recent estimates show that they cover 50,000 hectares in the Galápagos. At present, the national park is investigating methods to control these plants, but they remain the biggest challenge of all invasive species.

Solutions

In the past decade, efforts to eliminate invasive species have been stepped up, but it's no easy task. To prevent the situation from getting worse, the Galápagos Inspection and Quarantine System (SICGAL) organization checks all luggage and packages, both entering the islands and moving between islands, for organic materials of any kind. It may seem unnecessary to do this with foreign visitors, but even a piece of fruit could bring fruit flies onto the islands. The more rigorous checks and penalties for violations have discouraged the locals from importations and have led to confiscation of animals, plants, and seeds. Frustratingly, pets are still allowed, but they must be registered and neutered.

In terms of eliminating the species that are already on the islands, the best solution for larger animals is hunting, although with populations in the hundreds of thousands, it is costly and time-consuming. The alternatives are traps, which can ensnare other species, or poisoning, which is risky to the ecosystem. Hunting has reaped rewards, though in 2002, a four-year campaign succeeded in ridding Santiago Island of 25,000 feral pigs. Even more impressive has been the elimination of goats from Santiago, northern Isabela, and Floreana—over 250,000 bit the dust by 2006, and the campaign is ongoing to remove them from San Cristóbal and Santa Cruz. How the hunters achieved this monumental task was highly impressive. Goats were caught and fitted with radio-tracking collars, and their horns painted bright colors. When they were released and rejoined the herds, hunters shot them from helicopters, and the carcasses were left to rot.

There have been many other smaller-scale victories, but certain species, particularly rats, fire ants, and fruit trees, are proving far more difficult to control.

Regarding endangered species, progress is being made. Giant tortoise populations are being boosted by breeding centers on Santa Cruz, Floreana, San Cristóbal, and Isabela. In 2010, tortoises were reintroduced successfully to the remote island of Pinta, Lonesome George's original home. On Floreana, the population of dark-rumped petrels, which had been hunted to near extinction by dogs, cats, rats, and pigs, has recovered after a concerted effort to eliminate their predators. The endemic Floreana mockingbird is also being reintroduced to the island after its population had been confined to Champion Island.

While the conservationists are winning battles, redressing the balance of the archipelago's ecosystem is a long, hard war, and it will take many years to undo the damage invasive species have caused.

If you're interested in helping the Galápagos solve its environmental problems, tax-deductible **donations** for research, conservation, and environmental education can be sent to the **Charles Darwin Foundation** (407 N. Washington St., Suite 105, Falls Church, VA 22046, U.S. tel. 703/538-6833, darwin@galapagos.org, www.darwinfoundation.org) or the **Galápagos Conservation Trust** (5 Derby St., London W1Y 7AD, UK tel. 20/7629-5049, www.gct.org).

Flora and Fauna

It seems incredible that a set of rocky islands, parched in the equatorial sun and covered with blackened lava, could be teeming with so much life. However, it's precisely because of the inhospitable landscapes that creatures have been forced to adapt and, in doing so, provided the living proof for Darwin's theory of evolution.

The Galápagos has 5,000 species, and 1,900 are endemic: a third of the plants, almost half the birds, half the fish and insects, and 90 percent of the reptiles have all adapted so well to life in the archipelago that they barely resemble their original mainland ancestors.

Some 1,000 kilometers west of the South American mainland is a very long way to swim or fly, never mind crawl, so how on earth did the wildlife of the Galápagos come to be here? Nobody knows for sure, but it seems likely that the strengths of the ocean currents brought mammals such as sea lions to the archipelago, and they flourished in islands surrounded by waters teeming with marine life. Birds may have been blown off course, but more likely migratory birds came and knew they were on to a good thing, with an endless supply of fish, and returned year after year. Insects and plant seeds could also have been carried from the South American continent by high winds, whereas other seeds were probably excreted by birds or arrived stuck to their feet.

Explaining how terrestrial reptiles and rodents arrived is trickier, the most common theory being that they drifted on rafts of vegetation that still wash down Ecuador's oceanbound rivers. Any animals or plants that happened to be aboard, provided they could survive the journey, stood a slim chance of riding the currents all the way to the Galápagos. With their ability to slow their own metabolism, reptiles are particularly suited for such a long, difficult journey, while larger mammals would have died quickly, which explains the lack of mammals on the islands.

REPTILES

The Galápagos was named after the giant reptiles that inhabit them, and this is one of the only places on earth where reptiles rule the land with no natural predators. Thus the archipelago gives us a glimpse of what life might have been like millions of years ago when dinosaurs ruled the planet.

More than 90 percent of the reptile species in the Galápagos are endemic. In addition to the reptiles described below, the Galápagos harbors five endemic species of **gecko** and three species of **Galápagos snake.**

Giant Tortoises

Of the 20 species of endemic reptiles, these slow giants are the most famous. They also gave the islands their name—*galápago* is an old Spanish word for a saddle similar in shape to the tortoise shell. They are only found on the Galápagos and, in smaller numbers, on a few islands in the Indian Ocean. They reach sexual maturity at about 25 years and are not fully grown until age 100, reaching 1.5 meters in length and weighing up to 250 kilograms. Many live to the age of 160, although nobody knows their maximum age for sure.

The shell of a giant tortoise reveals which island its owner originates from. Saddle-shaped shells evolved on low, arid islands where tortoises needed to lift their heads high to eat tall vegetation, while semicircular domed shells come from higher lush islands where vegetation grows closer to the ground. The vice governor of the Galápagos boasted to Charles Darwin that he could distinguish the island of origin of a tortoise by the shape of its

© GALLO GUSZTAV/123RF

Giant tortoises can live more than 160 years.

shell—just one piece of evidence that helped Darwin to form his theory of evolution.

The tortoises' famous slow, languid demeanor is what allows them to live so long, and perhaps we should all take a cue from them and slow down a little. They spend 16 hours a day sleeping and are most active in the early morning and late afternoon. With minimal movement, their metabolism slows significantly, and digestion takes 1-3 weeks, allowing them to survive with very little food and water during the dry season. When the rains come, they come alive, eating, drinking, mating, wallowing in pools of water, and sleeping contentedly in large groups. They feed on a wide variety of plants, particularly opuntia cactus pads, fruits, water ferns, and bromeliads.

The only time tortoises make much noise is during mating season, when their unearthly groans echo for long distances. Males become surprisingly aggressive, pushing each other and rising up on their legs to stretch out their necks in a battle for dominance. The shorter male will usually retreat, while the larger male will ram a female's shell and nip her legs before mounting her from behind and bellowing. The process is long, arduous, and fraught with problems—males sometimes fall off and have great difficulty righting themselves.

When her eggs are ready to hatch, the female will journey for long distances to find dry sandy ground, usually on or near beaches, to dig a 30-centimeter-deep hole to bury the eggs, which hatch in the spring after about four months. The temperature of the nest has a marked effect on the gender of the hatchlings: Lower temperatures lead to more males and warmer temperatures more females.

Of the original 14 subspecies, 10 remain, and 3 species (Santa Fé, Floreana, and Fernandina) have been hunted into extinction. Indeed, the giant tortoise population has plummeted from some 250,000 before humans arrived to just 20,000 now. Sailors used to be the tortoises'

DID YOU KNOW . . . ?

- **Giant tortoises** are not fully grown until they are 100 years old. Many live to the age of 160, although nobody knows their maximum age for sure.

- **Flamingos** are born with gray plumage and slowly turn pink due to their shellfish-based diet. A brighter pink pigment is a sign of good health.

- When a **land iguana** nods its head, watch out; this is a territorial threat to other males, also employed against humans who get too close.

- **Blue-footed boobies** encircle their nests with a ring of excrement (guano). If the chick ventures outside the ring, it will often be rejected by its parents.

- **Marine iguanas** work hard to keep warm after staying underwater for more than an hour. On cold nights, they often congregate together into huge piles.

- **Booby** is a rude name for a bird, but not in the way you'd expect; it derives from *bobo*, meaning "stupid," in Spanish. It was coined by sailors derisive of the birds' friendly nature. Boobies are no chumps, though, and are very talented at fishing.

- Not all **finches** are cute. The sharp-billed ground finch is nicknamed "vampire finch" because it pecks at the base of a booby's tail to drink blood. It also rolls other birds' eggs until they break and then eats the insides.

- **Sea lion colonies** are split into harems where one dominant bull lives with up to 15 females, and bachelor colonies where other males congregate. Dominant bulls have to repel regular challenges and only last a few weeks or months before they are displaced by a stronger bull.

- **Frigates** and **penguins** are among the most romantic of Galápagos birds and usually mate for life; **albatross** are rather less romantic, many being polygamous during the mating season. The **Galápagos hawk** has the most unusual mating system, known as cooperative polyandry, whereby up to four males mate with a single female and then help to incubate and raise the young.

- **Albatross** can fly at speeds of 80 kilometers per hour and often spend years in flight without touching land.

main enemy, taking them on long voyages as sources of fresh meat (the tortoises took up to a year to starve to death). Today, the main danger comes largely from introduced species: Pigs dig up nests, cats eat hatchlings, and goats and cattle eat the vegetation and cut off the tortoises' food supply. It's not all bad news, however, because there is a comprehensive rearing program to release tortoises back into the wild, most recently on Pinta Island.

Five of the remaining subspecies are found on the five main volcanoes of Isabela, and the other species are found on Santiago, Santa Cruz, San Cristóbal, Pinzón, and Española.

Sea Turtles

There are four species of marine turtles in the archipelago. The eastern **Pacific green turtle,** known rather confusingly as *tortuga negra* (black turtle) in Spanish, is the most common species. Also present but rarely seen are the **Pacific leatherback,** the **Indo-Pacific hawksbill,** and the **olive ridley** turtles.

Green sea turtles are rarely seen in large numbers, preferring to swim alone, in couples, or next to their young. They usually weigh 100 kilograms but can weigh up to 150 kilograms. The females are bigger than the males and can grow to 1.2 meters long. They feed mainly on seaweeds and spend long periods of time submerged, even resting on the seabed and surviving without oxygen for several hours.

The mating season, November-January, is the best time to see them. Both genders are polygamous, and several males often mate with the same female. Mating is particularly tiring for the female, who has to do most of the swimming while the male holds on.

Sea turtles must come ashore to lay eggs, and females often do this as many as eight times during the mating season, laying dozens of eggs each time. The female climbs the beach above the high water mark and digs a pit to lay the eggs before returning to the sea. If the eggs can evade the attention of predators, particularly pigs, rats, and even crabs and beetles, then the hatchlings emerge and make their way to the sea, where they may be gobbled up by sharks or even pelicans.

Despite the high mortality rate, green sea turtles thrive in the islands and spread far from the archipelago. Turtles marked in the Galápagos have been found as far away as Panama and Costa Rica as well as commonly off the coast of Ecuador.

Marine Iguanas

The only seafaring lizards in the world, **Galápagos Marine Iguanas** are living proof of evolution. Scientists estimate that this species adapted over 2-3 million years from their land iguana cousins in order to find food underwater in the form of nutritious coastal seaweed. A flattened snout allows them to press against the rocks to feed, a flattened tail propels them more effectively underwater, long claws grab the rocks firmly, and salt-eliminating glands in their nostrils cleanse the sea salt from their bodies. The can dive more than 12 meters below the surface. They feed for an hour a day, always at low tide, and can stay underwater for more than an hour by lowering their heart rate by half.

The seaweed they feed on is true to its name—it's a weed that grows incredibly quickly throughout the coastline of the islands and supports more than 200,000 marine iguanas on the Galápagos. Males measure about one meter

> # TRAVELS WITH CHARLIE
>
> When in the water this lizard swims with perfect ease and quickness, by a serpentine movement of its body and flattened tail – the legs being motionless and closely collapsed on its sides. A seaman on board sank one, with a heavy weight attached to it, thinking thus to kill it directly; but when, an hour afterwards, he drew up the line, it was quite active.
>
> Charles Darwin in *The Voyage of the Beagle*, on marine iguanas

in length and weigh up to 20 kilograms. They are mostly black, with red and green tinges on their backs becoming particularly prominent during the mating season.

After feeding, regulating its body heat fills much of the rest of the marine iguana's day. After a long dive, they must warm up, but not too quickly and not to more than 45°C. To do so, iguanas face the sun, exposing as little surface area as possible, and raise their bodies off the ground to allow air to circulate underneath-they often look like they're striking a yoga pose. On cold days and at night, iguanas congregate into huge piles to conserve heat.

Marine iguanas congregate in colonies for most of the year. During the mating season, which usually corresponds with the rainy season, males become more brightly colored, and their black coloring is punctuated by red, orange, and green spots. Males become more territorial and aggressive, standing proudly and bobbing their heads up and down rapidly to warn off other males. This head-bobbing is also used to court females. After mating, females lay their eggs in sandy burrows on beaches, and hatchlings emerge after three or four months.

Young ones and even slow elderly iguanas have one predator to fear: the Galápagos hawk.

Like much of the wildlife on the archipelago, iguanas were affected by El Niño conditions in the 1980s and 1990s, when abnormally warm waters killed the shallow-growing seaweed. The marine iguanas were not strong enough to dive deeper, and thousands perished. Their numbers have slowly recovered, but who knows if they will evolve further over time to become better divers?

Land Iguanas

The Galápagos have seven subspecies of land iguana. How they arrived on the island is the cause of much debate—they may have floated on vegetation from the South American coast—but they almost certainly came after their marine cousins, when there was enough vegetation on the islands for them to survive on land. They live in dry areas and eat anything from berries, flowers, fruits, and cactus pads, ingesting most of their water from food. Like their marine cousins, newborns are one of the few terrestrial creatures that have to fear the Galápagos hawk. They are also prey for many introduced species until they are big enough to defend themselves. As a result, the land iguana species on Santiago and Baltra are extinct, while those on other islands are endangered. A captive-breeding program at the Darwin Center is working to boost the population.

Males grow to over one meter in length, can weigh up to 13 kilograms, and live more than 50 years. The Galápagos species are distinctively more yellow than greener mainland iguanas, particularly the subspecies on Santa Fé. There are also hybrids born from mating with marine iguanas.

Like their marine cousins, the males can be very territorial, exhibiting brighter colors in the mating season and engaging in head-bashing battles with other males. They are famous for their head-nodding, a threat that can also be employed against humans if they get too close. Note that male iguanas can also whip their tails up if startled, so be careful approaching them. They are also surprisingly fast and can run across the rocks at high speeds. Females need to be fast too as males are extremely persistent in attempting to mate, employing the same head-nodding movement and chasing them for long periods of time. The female is considerably smaller and so often unable to resist advances, during which the male holds her neck and hooks a leg over her to bring his tail in contact with hers. After mating, the female lays eggs in burrows, and hatchlings emerge after three or four months. Hatchlings need to avoid the attention of herons, egrets, hawks, and owls, but once they grow, they have no natural predators.

Lava Lizards

Although hardly as impressive as their larger relatives, the seven species of lava lizard are certainly faster—and they have to be to avoid being gobbled up by birds or snakes. You'll see them scurrying over sand and rocks all over the islands. They have various other evasive techniques—changing color to camouflage themselves, and leaving a breakaway tail in predators' mouths while they make a getaway and grow a new one. They feed on insects, plants, and occasionally each other. The males can often be seen doing a type of push-up as a show of strength, and their Spanish name (*lagartija*) has become a common slang term for this type of exercise.

Other Reptiles

On land, there are three species of **snakes** on the islands; all are brown and feed on rats, geckos, lava lizards, and marine iguana hatchlings. They are venomous but rarely seen by humans, and there have been no reports of bites. Underwater, the yellow-bellied sea snake is also venomous. At night, **geckos** come out to feed

© FABIO IACOPONI/123RF

A lava lizard perches atop a marine iguana on Fernandina.

on insects and spend their days resting under rocks. Like lava lizards, they can lose their tails and regenerate them easily.

MAMMALS

In contrast to the abundance of plants, insects, fish, and lizards, the Galápagos has only six types of mammals—sea lions, fur seals, whales, and dolphins, all of which must have swum to the archipelago. There are also bats, which flew over, and most impressive of all, rice rats, which most likely arrived by floating on rafts of vegetation.

Galápagos Sea Lions

A close encounter with sea lions is for many people the highlight of a Galápagos trip. While other creatures show a mild disdain for humans, sea lions are very communicative and the pups are particularly playful in the water, which makes for an incredible snorkeling experience. They seem to delight in playing impromptu games of peekaboo and demonstrating their acrobatic skills underwater. After a hard day's fishing and playing, the sea lions sprawl over beaches and rocks, snoozing to replenish their oxygen supplies. Walking among a colony is another highlight of any trip. Outside their colonies, they are often found dozing on boats and docks.

However, they are not called lions for nothing (or "wolves" in Spanish—*lobos marineros*). The mature males can reach 2.5 meters in length, considerably bigger than the females, and they are more than a little scary. Males mate with about 10-15 females and can be very territorial, so be advised that although most of this posturing is harmless, sea lions occasionally attack—it's the principal cause of animal injury to visitors in the Galápagos. Steer well clear of patrolling males, especially when snorkeling. Their behavior is understandable, though—with such an uneven ratio of cows to bulls, many bulls are left fending for themselves and plotting their next move, and territorial battles are common. There are several bachelor colonies in the archipelago, where surplus males congregate. Dominant bulls are soon tired out, and territory tenure ranges from a few days to a few months before a new bull comes along and makes a successful challenge.

Mating usually takes place in shallow water or on land. Females give birth to a single pup, which is suckled for 1-3 years. The pups often congregate in "nurseries" while the adults are out fishing. Pups rarely swim without adults until they begin to fish for themselves, at about five months. The adults continue to accompany them, mindful that they do not swim too far out and attract predators in the form of sharks and killer whales.

Unfortunately, the sea lion population has declined considerably in recent years due to a lack of fish after the 1998 El Niño, but there are still more than 25,000 in the archipelago. Females live to age 20, and males slightly less.

Galápagos Fur Seal

Smaller than sea lions and with a thick, furry coat, the Galápagos fur seal are also harder to see because they prefer shaded areas and cooler waters. We are lucky that these endearing animals with their bearlike snouts and small external ears exist at all after they were hunted to the brink of extinction in the 19th century. The warm two-layered pelt was in high demand in Europe and the United States, leading to slaughter on a mass scale.

The seal population recovered slowly through the 20th century but has suffered at the hands of nature as well as people. The warm currents of the El Niño phenomenon were particularly devastating, killing their supply of fish. Although they are endemic to the islands, many seals have now emigrated to the coast of Peru. There are still estimated to be over 20,000 fur seals inhabiting the northern and western islands of Pinta, Marchena, Santiago, Isabela, and Fernandina. The social behavior and breeding of fur seals is very similar to sea lions, although bulls establish their territory on land in contrast to sea lions, which tend to defend it from the sea.

Fur seals' preference for cooler water also puts them at greater risk from sharks that inhabit these waters, and attacks are frequent.

Whales and Dolphins

The mammals that pop in and out of the water are far easier to see than the several cetaceans (completely aquatic mammals) that live in the waters around the archipelago. There are many species of whales, but it's rare to see them. The massive blue whale is an occasional visitor, but you're more likely to spot humpback whales breaching. The killer whales or orcas are the most feared, preying on sea lions and fur seals. The often swim in small groups and are known to use sonar to locate their prey. Far more commonly seen are schools of bottlenose dolphins surfing the bow waves of cruise boats and leaping in unison.

Bats

Two endemic species of bats made the long crossing from the South American mainland—probably by accident—to settle in the Galápagos. They roost in trees and mangroves, feeding on insects.

Rats

Two species of rice rats are left from the original seven that must have arrived floating on vegetation. The rest have been driven to extinction by the larger Norway rat that was introduced by visiting ships and remains a major threat to native species. The two species are found on Fernandina and Santa Fé. They feed mainly on seeds and vegetation.

SEABIRDS

Surrounded by water rich in fish, it's no surprise that the Galápagos is teeming with birdlife. Only a small minority of species—5 out of 19—are endemic: the Galápagos penguin, flightless cormorant, waved albatross, lava gull, and swallow-tailed gull. The other species, including the boobies and frigates that receive a lot of attention from visitors, are found elsewhere in Ecuador and the South American coast.

Boobies

The Spanish sailors who first discovered the Galápagos were very unimpressed by a bird that would simply peer at them curiously instead of fleeing, so they called these birds *bobos* (stupid), and the name stuck. *Amigos* would have been nicer and more appropriate for these amenable birds, who are completely unfazed by humans walking within a meter or two of them on island trails. The insult to their intelligence is particularly unfair because boobies are no

Boobies are highly skilled at fishing. You'll see them dive-bombing the ocean at high speeds to secure their meals.

© DR. LOUISE WESTWOOD

chumps—they are astonishingly adept at catching fish, dive-bombing the waters from as high as 25 meters before popping up to the surface and gulping down the luckless prey. The shock of the impact with the sea is diffused by air sacs in the boobies' skulls.

The **blue-footed boobies** are the most commonly seen because they nest on the ground. There are actually far more **red-footed boobies** in the archipelago, but these smaller birds tend to feed farther out to sea and are mainly found on the more remote islands. In contrast to the other species, they nest in trees and shrubs. The **masked boobies** are the largest booby, with a wingspan of 1.5 meters. They nest on cliff edges, finding it difficult to take off from level ground. They are named for the black eye mask that contrasts with their bright white plumage.

If you're lucky enough to see blue-footed booby's mating ritual, it's hilarious: The male marches around, kicking his feet up high, then raises his beak skyward, whistles, and opens his wings as if to say, "How can you resist my bright-blue feet?" The bluer the better, in the female's view, who responds with a honk if she likes what she sees. After mating, the couple often begins to build a nest together, 1-3 eggs are laid, and the couple takes turns incubating them for about 40 days.

After hatching, the nest area is surrounded by a ring of excrement called guano. If the chick ventures outside the ring, it will often be rejected and could end up as lunch for a hawk or frigate. The male does most of the fishing, and females also help out, but only when the chicks are large enough to defend themselves.

Frigate Birds

If you're a frigate bird, size clearly matters. These scavengers are most famous for the bright red chest pouches that males inflate to the size of a basketball to attract females in the mating season. Once inflated, the male spends the entire day that way, calling and flapping his wings at passing females, hoping to attract one to the nest he has built for her. It's particularly romantic because once the female chooses the best-chested male, they mate for life. The sight of the inflated pouches is one of the highlights of bird-watching on the archipelago.

After mating a single egg is laid, and both parents share the incubation duties for 7-8 weeks. After hatching, the young have to wait five months before they are able to fly and learn from their parents how to scavenge. Frigates don't reach maturity until age five.

Mating aside, though, frigates are actually the bad guys of the archipelago; they are scavengers that live mainly by stealing food from other birds. There are two species of frigates on the islands: the great and the magnificent, very similar in appearance, and both have the famous red sacs. They have a wide wingspan that can reach over two meters, but they are unable to swim. Instead, they harass other birds, particularly boobies, into coughing up their hard-earned meal in an unpleasant show of avian bullying; sometimes they even steal fish right out of a chick's mouth. However, they are also very resourceful and sometimes catch flying fish from just above the surface. Frigates have also learned that humans are a good source of food and are often seen following fishing boats in the hope of scavenging scraps.

Waved Albatross

If you don't go to Española, you probably won't see the largest seabird in the archipelago—it's as simple as that. Nearly the entire world population of waved albatross nests on this island April-November before migrating to Peru. With a wingspan of 2.5 meters, it is quite a sight to see them taking off and landing. Española gets so busy in mating season that landing areas, most famously Punta Suárez, are nicknamed "albatross airports." Once they're out of the skies, these graceful fliers become surprisingly awkward; they often fall over after landing and then waddle around clumsily. It's not a surprise when you consider that many birds have not walked on land for months, even years, without actually "landing," only leaving the skies to float on water far out in the ocean.

True to the Galápagos tradition, like boobies and frigates, albatross have an entertaining mating ritual. The couples perform an elaborate courtship display, clacking their bills together, sky calling, and dancing around in a synchronized, circular walk. They sometimes do this for several hours, and the island turns into a kind of open-air avian disco. However, albatross are not the faithful birds we once thought they were, and recent research has shown that some have several partners while others are monogamous.

The first birds arrive on Española at the end of March, and courtship reaches its peak in April. The egg is incubated by both parents for two months. The birds quite often move the egg around rather than staying in one nest. The first chicks arrive in June-July, and the adults feed them regurgitated fish oils until they are old enough to fly, usually by the end of the year, when they migrate.

Albatross can live up to age 50, and when not breeding, they spend their time at sea, sitting on the surface of the ocean to feed on squid and fish.

Galápagos Penguins

The last thing you'd expect to see on the equator is a penguin, and these endearing little birds are special in two ways—they are the only penguin found in the northern hemisphere (the equator cuts across the north of Isabela), and at just 35 centimeters tall they are one of the smallest penguins in the world. They evolved from the Humboldt penguins that inhabit the coast of Chile but have retained much of their original insulation. So while other species like iguanas and sea lions warm up on the rocks, the penguins struggle to cool down by swimming, standing with their wings out at 45-degree angles, and even panting rapidly. They rise early and spend most of the day swimming and fishing before returning to their colonies in the afternoon. You're most likely to see them standing around on the rocks, but in the water they are quite a sight-streaking after fish at speeds up to 40 kilometers per hour.

Galápagos penguins molt once a year, usually just before breeding, and during this period they do not enter the water. The penguins usually mate for life and lay eggs in crevices, caves, or holes to keep them out of the sun. The parents guard the eggs for five weeks until they hatch. Penguins do have to fear aquatic predators, but the main threat in recent years has been starvation. The 1998 El Niño had a severe effect on penguin numbers, and the latest estimates put the population at less than 2,000.

Flightless Cormorants

Flightless Cormorants are proof that evolution is not all about gaining skills but also about losing them. These birds spend so much time in water, and with no predators to fear on land, they have lost their ability to fly, the only species of cormorant to have done so. They have neither the chest muscles nor the wing span to take to the air but instead have long necks, strong kicking legs, and webbed feet that make them experts at catching fish, eels, and even octopuses underwater.

They have an unusual courtship ritual, although you're unlikely to see it as it takes place underwater. The pair performs an aquatic "dance," swimming back and forth past each other before the male leads the female to the surface to mate. They build nests of seaweed on rocks and beaches very close to the waterline—so close that some are washed away by high tides. Two or three eggs are laid, and incubation takes about 35 days.

Endemic Gulls

There are over 35,000 **swallow-tailed gulls** nesting throughout the archipelago. These attractive birds sport a black head, a distinctive red eye ring, a white-and-gray body, and red feet. Unlike most gulls, swallowtails feed nocturnally, leave at dusk, and help to point boat captains toward land at dawn. The **lava gull** is thought to be the rarest gull in the world, with only 400 mating pairs nesting exclusively in the Galápagos. Their dark-gray plumage makes them difficult to pick out from the lava rocks they inhabit.

Other Seabirds

Elsewhere in the world a pelican swooping into the sea to catch fish is considered an impressive sight. Here on the Galápagos, **brown pelicans** don't get as much attention as the more colorful and rarer birdlife. They are amazing creatures, though, filling their enormous 14-liter beak pouches on impact with the ocean, filtering out the fish, and gulping them down.

Red-billed tropic birds feed far out to sea and return to their nests on windy cliff-sides. They have a gray-and-white body and long flowing white pin-tails capped by a distinctive red bill and a black mask.

COASTAL BIRDS

While they don't get nearly as much attention as their seafaring cousins, the islands' coastal and land birds are still fascinating, not least to Charles Darwin. One of the many mysteries of the Galápagos is how land birds that cannot fly over the sea could have arrived here; the most plausible conclusion is that they were blown all the way from the mainland by storms.

Herons and Egrets

There are five species of herons, all prolific hunters of small lizards, rodents, insects, and fish. They stand motionless as statues and spear their prey with their long beaks. The largest is the **great blue heron,** 1.5 meters tall; the smaller **yellow-crowned night heron** feeds by night. The only endemic species is the small gray **lava heron** that hunts in rock pools.

Greater Flamingos

Their distinctive pink makes these birds an attractive sight in the lagoons around the archipelago. They feed on shrimp by filtering through the salty lagoon water, and it is this shellfish diet that turns them pink from their original white.

Migrant Species

Six species of birds come down to the archipelago during winter in the northern hemisphere. They are the **semipalmated plover,** the **ruddy turnstone,** the **wandering tattler,** the **sanderling,** the **whimbrel,** and the **northern phalarope.**

LAND BIRDS
Mockingbirds

There are four species of mockingbirds endemic to the Galápagos, feeding mainly on insects and small reptiles. Sadly, though, mockingbirds are increasingly endangered due to introduced species, such as rats and cats, that hunt the chicks. Adults also need their wits about them to avoid the Galápagos hawk. They are slowly being reintroduced to Floreana following a large-scale extermination of invasive species.

Galápagos Hawks

Out of the water, this fearless bird is the largest natural predator on the islands. It eats everything from baby iguanas and lizards to small birds, rodents, and insects as well as scavenging on dead animals. It also has a highly unusual mating system known as cooperative polyandry: Up to four males mate with a single female, and then help incubate and raise the young.

TRAVELS WITH CHARLIE

I have seen one of the thick-billed finches picking at one end of a piece of cactus whilst a lizard was eating at the other end; and afterwards the little bird with the utmost indifference hopped on the back of the reptile.

Charles Darwin in *The Voyage of the Beagle,* on the fearlessness of finches

---

Darwin Finches

From a scientific viewpoint, these tiny birds are arguably the most important species in the Galápagos. The 13 species of finches with varied beak shapes were the most important inspiration for Charles Darwin's evolution theory. The key to the finches' survival, as Darwin noted, is the beak. Short, thick beaks enable **ground finches** to crack hard seeds, while longer, slimmer bills allow other species to probe crevices for insects and eat cacti or flowers. The finches obviously came from a common ancestor, but they are subtly different according to which island and even which part of the island they inhabit.

Finches are remarkably resourceful birds and are one of the few species to use tools to find prey. **Woodpecker** and **mangrove finches** use a cactus spine or small twig to get at grubs burrowed deep in tree branches.

The **sharp-billed ground finch** is the most unusual species, and a little sinister. It is nicknamed the "vampire finch" for its habit of pecking at the base of a booby's tail until it can drink a trickle of blood. The boobies offer

© MORTEN ELM/123RF

a finch on Santa Cruz Island

little resistance, perhaps because the pecking also helps to remove parasites. This species also rolls other birds' eggs until they break and then eats the insides.

One aspect that unites the many species of finches is that they all have to fear the Galápagos hawk.

Other Land Birds

Other notable species include the beautiful but easily startled **Galápagos dove** (*Zenaida galapagoensis*), which has pink, gray, and white plumage, red feet, and a blue eye ring. The male **vermillion flycatcher** deserves special mention for its fiery red plumage, as does the **yellow warbler,** whose sunshine plumage is as beautiful as its songs.

MARINE LIFE

The temperatures of the waters around the Galápagos are the foundation on which most life is built. These temperatures are as diverse as

the wildlife, varying from a bone-chilling 15°C to near-thermal bath comfort of 30°C. With such a wide range of temperatures and depths, some 300 fish species inhabit the waters, which makes the Galápagos a wonderful snorkeling and diving destination. Snorkelers and divers can often gaze into a school of fish that seems to go on forever.

Sharks

While there are few natural predators on land in the Galápagos, underwater is a different story. The cold waters are ideal for sharks, so sea lions have to be careful when swimming too far out. Luckily for humans, these sharks are mainly harmless. The most common are the docile **white-tipped sharks** and **black-tipped sharks,** who eat plankton and small fish. They tend to rest under rocks and in caves but are also commonly seen swimming close to shore.

For the more adventurous, watch for scary-looking **hammerhead sharks.** Large schools of 30-40 of these incredible creatures are commonly encountered when diving, although they can occasionally be seen while snorkeling at Kicker Rock (León Dormido) or off the north shore of Floreana.

The largest shark in the archipelago is the huge **whale shark,** up to 20 meters long, found only at the outlying islands of Darwin and Wolf, visited mainly by dedicated dive boats.

Rays

Encountering a school of rays gliding along flapping their wings like underwater birds is unforgettable, and the Galápagos is filled with these beautiful creatures. When they swim past you, it's a highlight of any snorkeling or diving excursion, and on occasion they can also be viewed from boats. The most common are the **stingrays,** whose wings can span up to 1.8 meters, but be careful of the sting, which can whip up if you startle them. They are also found resting on sandy beaches, so watch where you step. More spectacular are the brightly colored **golden rays;** the massive **manta rays,** an incredible six meters across; and the rarer **spotted eagle rays,** found mainly in deeper waters.

Fish

Choosing highlights from the vast array of fish in the waters around the archipelago is tricky, but top of the list are the multicolored **parrot fish;** the **clown fish,** of *Finding Nemo* fame; the **moorish idol,** with its long dorsal fin over a body banded with black, yellow, and white; and the orange, black, and white **harlequin wrasse,** a hermaphrodite that can spontaneously change sex from female to male.

Crustaceans and Other Marine Life

Nobody expects crabs to be a highlight of a Galápagos trip, but you'll be surprised at how eye-catching some of the invertebrates are. Of

Sally lightfoot crabs are an unexpected highlight.

the 100 crab species in the islands, most colorful is the bright-red **sally lightfoot crab,** named for its fast movement across water over short distances. They are easily startled and can give a nasty pinch. They need to be fast to avoid the attentions of herons and moray eels. Other invertebrate species of note include **pencil-spined sea urchins,** many neon-colored species of **starfish,** and the increasingly rare **sea cucumbers,** which have been harvested for their medicinal benefits and are now an endangered species.

ARTHROPODS

This diverse range of species includes beetles, flies, spiders, ants, bees, wasps, butterflies, moths, grasshoppers, scorpions, ticks, and centipedes. There are 1,600 species of insects in the islands, but unlike in the Ecuadorian rainforest, they are far harder to see (most are nocturnal) and not nearly as interesting. Of the ants, the worst are the invasive species of **fire ants,** which eat the eggs of birds, iguanas, and tortoises as well as fruits that are the source of food for many endemic species on the islands. The solitary species of bee is the **carpenter bee,** essential for pollination.

FLORA

With such a bewildering array of wildlife and rugged volcanic landscapes to keep visitors busy, the plants of the Galápagos don't get much attention, and you're more likely to notice the absence of vegetation than its presence in often barren terrain. To put this in perspective, mainland Ecuador has 25,000 species of plants, while the Galápagos has only 550 species, only a third of which are endemic. However, the rainy season leads to an explosion of greenery on the larger islands, and there is much to admire in the hills.

The habitat of Galápagos plants is spread across three diverse areas: the coastal or littoral area, where fresh highland water meets saltwater; the semideserts of the dry areas; and the lush, humid, misty highland area.

Mangroves

The coastal areas' flora is dominated by tangled mangroves, consisting of trees and plants that can only grow in brackish water. They weave themselves into the sand and send up small breathing roots called pneumatophores. The archipelago has four types: the **red mangrove,** found along sheltered shores and on the edges of lagoons, is the most common, with larger, pointier, shinier leaves; the paler **white mangrove;** the darker **black mangrove,** found on sandy beaches; and the less common **button mangrove.**

Palo Santo Trees

In the dry areas, the lifeless-looking *palo santo* tree blankets the landscapes. They may not look like much, but the smell of the wood is

Opuntia cacti are a food supply for many species on the archipelago.

famously aromatic, used throughout Ecuador both as incense in church and to repel mosquitoes. The trees were given their name, which translates as "holy wood," for their habit of flowering near Christmas.

Cacti

Even more prevalent in dry areas are various species of cacti. The **opuntia** prickly pear cactus has evolved into 14 separate species throughout the archipelago. True to the Galápagos tradition, the species evolved according to which predator they have to repel. On islands with large populations of land iguanas and tortoises, the cacti are taller and thicker with stronger spines, growing up to 12 meters high. On islands with no large predators, opuntia cacti grow low to the ground, and their spines are soft enough for birds to nest in and pollinate the cactus in return. Other Galápagos cacti include the endemic **lava cactus,** often the first thing to grow in new lava flows, and the more impressive **candelabra cactus,** whose branches stretch up to seven meters across.

Other Flora

The highlands of Santiago, Santa Cruz, San Cristóbal, and Floreana contain the richest variety of plantlife. Here you'll find dense forests of *lechoso* **trees,** a world away from the barren lowlands below. There are 90 species of **ferns,** some of which grow up to three meters, and an equal number of mosses. **Orchids,** an endemic species of **mistletoe,** the purple and pink *cacotillo,* and purple-and-white **passion**

flowers bring splashes of color to the highlands. Charles Darwin, of course, had a flower named after him—**Darwin's aster,** whose tiny white blossoms can be seen in highland grass.

A rare edible endemic plant is the **Galápagos tomato,** which produce small green, yellow, and red fruits. There are 300 species of **lichens** on the islands, a symbiosis of algae and fungi. These lichens produce dyes ranging from purple, red, and orange to green and gray. Production of purple **dyer's moss** was a focus of some penal colonies on the islands in the early 20th century, but it was very labor intensive and not particularly lucrative.

History

The Galápagos Islands' isolation and inhospitable volcanic terrain have been their greatest assets for much of their history, saving them from colonization and degradation until relatively recently. With the South American coast 1,000 kilometers to the east and nothing but blue Pacific Ocean all the way to French Polynesia, over 5,000 kilometers to the west, the Galápagos really was a hidden jewel for centuries.

EARLY VISITORS

It's not clear who the first visitors to the islands were, but it's probable that they were sailors blown off course or people on hapless fishing boats blown out to sea. Most of them were likely unimpressed by the lack of freshwater on the islands. Whether the Incas ever made it here is disputed; in 1572, Spanish chronicler Miguel Sarmiento de Gamboa claimed that the Inca Túpac Yupanqui had visited the archipelago, but there is little evidence for this, and many experts consider it a far-fetched legend, especially since the Incas weren't seafaring people.

The discovery of the islands by Europeans was officially made in 1535, when the ship of

Tomás de Berlanga, Bishop of Panama, was pushed off course by the Panama Current on its way to Peru. The crew didn't stay long, but the bishop wrote to King Charles V of Spain enthusing about the giant tortoises with shells shaped like riding saddles (called *galápagos* in Spanish), and the name stuck. The islands appeared on a 1574 world map with the label "Insulae de los Galopegos." The islands were given their pseudonym, Las Islas Encantadas (The Enchanted Islands), by Spanish conquistador Diego de Rivadeneira, who believed the islands to be enchanted, moving with the ocean's currents; it made a better story than his navigation being a little off.

PIRATES AND WHALERS

During the 17th century, the Galápagos were used as a base for Dutch, French, and English pirates, most famously Sir Francis Drake, to mount raids on coastal ports and treasure-filled Spanish galleons. The pirate William Ambrose Cowley made the first working map of the Galápagos, naming islands after British royalty and aristocracy. Floreana and Santiago Islands were originally called Charles and

James, respectively, after British monarchs, and Isabela was once called Albemarle after a duke of the same title.

Given pirates' propensity to plunder, it's no surprise that they were the first humans to cause damage to the islands' ecosystem. The pirates realized the value of taking a giant tortoise on long voyages to provide fresh meat. Thousands were taken and stowed in ships' holds, enduring a slow death over the course of a year without food or water. This was the beginning of the drastic reduction in the giant tortoise population that had been over 250,000 before human arrival. Fur seals were another target, sold for their pelts, and by the early 19th century it became clear that the Galápagos was far more valuable than had previously been thought. On February 12, 1832, the newly independent Ecuador fought off halfhearted claims by the United States and Britain to claim the islands officially.

CHARLES DARWIN AND THE GALÁPAGOS

Just three years after Ecuador claimed the archipelago, a young British scientist named Charles Darwin, then just age 26, visited aboard the HMS *Beagle.* Darwin collected crucial evidence, particularly from the many species of finches, that helped formulate his theory of evolution, published in *The Origin of Species* in 1859. This monumental work forever changed human beings' view of life on earth.

Charles Robert Darwin was born in Shropshire, England, in 1809 to an upper-middle-class British family. His father was a doctor and determined that his son would follow him into the profession, but Charles had other ideas, collecting specimens and studying botany in his spare time. He neglected his medical studies in Edinburgh in favor of his fascination for nature, and when his father transferred him to Cambridge to study theology, Darwin

TRAVELS WITH CHARLIE

While staying in the upper region, we lived entirely upon tortoise-meat: the breast-plate roasted, with the flesh on it, is very good; and the young tortoises make excellent soup; but otherwise the meat to my taste is indifferent.

Charles Darwin in *The Voyage of the Beagle;* even the renowned ecologist had a hand in the reduction of the giant tortoise population.

developed an interest in philosophical works on creation and adaptation.

Soon after graduating, Darwin was thrilled to be given the post of unpaid naturalist aboard the HMS *Beagle,* a small sailing vessel that left Plymouth, England, on December 27, 1831. The *Beagle* landed twice off the coast of Africa before crossing the Atlantic and beginning a two-year exploration of South America's eastern coast. Darwin explored the forests of Brazil and the high plains of Uruguay before the *Beagle* rounded Cape Horn in 1834 and headed up the western coast of Chile and Peru.

Darwin arrived in the Galápagos in September 1835 and spent five weeks here, visiting San Cristóbal, Floreana, Santiago, and Isabela. The evidence of evolution was everywhere—the different shapes of finch's beaks, iguanas that had learned to swim, and cormorants that no longer needed to fly. The governor of the archipelago remarked to Darwin that he could identify which island a giant tortoise was from by the shape of its shell, and Darwin was particularly struck by the variation in mockingbirds caught on different islands. But far from having a eureka moment, Darwin took samples

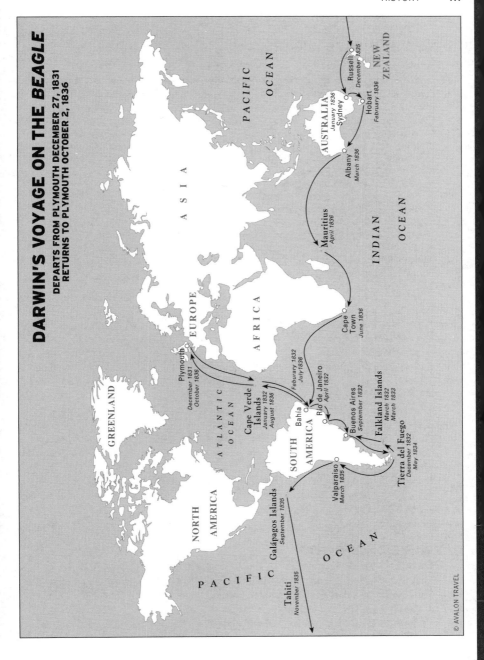

DARWIN'S VOYAGE ON THE BEAGLE

DEPARTS FROM PLYMOUTH DECEMBER 27, 1831
RETURNS TO PLYMOUTH OCTOBER 2, 1836

TRAVELS WITH CHARLIE

The natural history of these islands is eminently curious, and well deserves attention. Most of the organic productions are aboriginal creations, found nowhere else; there is even a difference between the inhabitants of the different islands; yet all show a marked relationship with those of America, though separated from that continent by an open space of ocean, between 500 and 600 miles in width. The archipelago is a little world within itself, or rather a satellite attached to America, whence it has derived a few stray colonists, and has received the general character of its indigenous productions. Considering the small size of the islands, we feel the more astonished at the number of their aboriginal beings, and at their confined range. Seeing every height crowned with its crater, and the boundaries of most of the lava-streams still distinct, we are led to believe that within a period geologically recent the unbroken ocean was here spread out. Hence, both in space and time, we seem to be brought somewhat near to that great fact – that mystery of mysteries – the first appearance of new beings on this earth.

Charles Darwin in *The Voyage of the Beagle,* realizing how vital the Galápagos was to his work on evolution

of species from as many islands as he could and took copious quantities of notes, which he analyzed for years afterward.

Even though he was a naturalist, he didn't take to all of the species he encountered, being particularly scathing about the marine iguanas, calling them "most disgusting clumsy lizards." Darwin was similar in his behavior to other sailors and wrote of his experience enjoying giant tortoise meat ("The breast plate roasted with the meat on it is very good") and the less enjoyable taste of iguana meat ("These lizards, when cooked, yield a white meat, which is liked by those whose stomachs soar above all prejudices.").

DARWIN'S THEORY OF EVOLUTION

Darwin returned to England in October 1836. His visit to the Galápagos had changed him fundamentally. He had embarked on the *Beagle* voyage a firm believer in the biblical story of creation and the idea that God created perfect, immutable creatures. But the evidence of so many variations of subspecies on the islands was undeniable—why else did one finch have a slightly longer beak on an island where its primary food source were insects living in crevices, while another finch had a shorter, stronger beak better for cracking nuts? The only logical explanation was that the finch species had adapted to their environment. Darwin was a meticulous and devout man, and it took him more than 20 years to finally publish his findings. A key reason for the delay was his concern over the impact of his theory on Victorian England's highly evangelical society. In the end, the threat of someone else publishing the theory first finally spurred him to act: A fellow naturalist, Alfred Russel Wallace—younger and less conventional than Darwin—was about to publish a similar theory in 1858. When Darwin's friends discovered this, they arranged for Darwin and Wallace to read a joint paper to the Linnean Society of London, formally

© BEN WESTWOOD

According to philosopher Daniel Dennett, Charles Darwin had "the single best idea anyone has ever had."

the ones best-suited to their environment survived to reproduce.

> As many more individuals of each species are born than can possibly survive; and as, consequently, there is a frequently recurring struggle for existence, it follows that any being, if it vary however slightly in any manner profitable to itself, under the complex and sometimes varying conditions of life, will have a better chance of surviving, and thus be naturally selected. From the strong principle of inheritance, any selected variety will tend to propagate its new and modified form.

The process could even work in "reverse," leading to the loss of adaptations that were suddenly no longer beneficial. On an island with no predators, and hence no need to fly to safety, wings might eventually just get in the way. Birds that could somehow forgo growing them would be able to swim after fish more efficiently and have more energy left over for other things—such as reproduction—than their fellows; thus the cormorant became flightless. The theory applied not just to physical attributes but also to behavior. Birds surrounded by predators would be naturally timid, while birds on the Galápagos, with no natural predators, were uncommonly docile.

presenting evolution to the public for the first time. To this day, Wallace is credited as the codiscoverer of natural selection.

On November 24, 1859, Darwin published *On the Origin of Species by Means of Natural Selection,* and the world would never be quite the same. The book's central idea, while being revolutionary to Victorian England, was extremely simple—that organisms change over time in order to adapt to the challenges presented in their habitats. One of the biggest inspirations for the idea was the beak shapes of Galápagos finches. This idea became the cornerstone of the concept of the process of natural selection. To explain the process, Darwin proposed a mechanism called descent with modification. He based it on observations of animals and plants in captivity, which produced many more offspring than their environmental "niche" could possibly support. Only

Darwin was the first to admit that his theory was still full of holes, and that he was not the first to suggest this concept, having drawn on the work of a long list of scientists, including Jean-Baptiste Lamarck, Charles Lyell, Thomas Malthus, and Darwin's own grandfather, Erasmus. But his modesty did nothing to quell the uproar that it caused in Victorian England, just as he had feared it would. The church was particularly unhappy at Darwin's implication that God's work was not perfect but had to be changed over time. Darwin, who had recently been bereaved by the death of his infant son from scarlet fever, was suffering from illness that kept him away from public events and out of the storm. He remained a committed Christian and fervently disagreed that his theory was at odds with belief in God.

However, with the support of friends and scientific colleagues, toward the end of his life Darwin's theory gradually became accepted, and nowadays it is accepted as scientific fact. Darwin continued his work into old age, publishing several more books, and lived out the remainder of his days with his wife and 10 children in Downe House in Kent. He died on April 19, 1882, at age 73. He was given a state funeral, a rare honor outside the royal family, and buried in Westminster Abbey next to Sir Isaac Newton.

THE EARLY 20TH CENTURY

These so-called "enchanted islands" became anything but through the latter part of the 19th century, when most of the residents were convicts. Similar to the British policy of sending convicts to Australia, Ecuador commuted the death penalty to a life sentence toiling on the islands, enduring cruel treatment and scratching out a meager existence, such as by making dye from lichen. There were colonies on Floreana, San Cristóbal, and Isabela, the latter functioning until 1959.

As the world plunged into World War II, the Galápagos was used by the U.S. Navy to protect the entrance to the new Panama Canal, completed in 1914. After the war, the first permanent settlers (apart from the convicts) began to arrive, among them the Wittmer family. During World War II, the U.S. Army Air Forces set up an airport on Baltra to monitor Japanese activity in the South Pacific, and then donated the airport to Ecuador after the war.

DEATH IN PARADISE: THE GALÁPAGOS AFFAIR

By the early 20th century, the world had woken up to the wonders of the Galápagos, and it was only a matter of time before Europeans were attracted to escape to a place depicted in books and newspapers as a slice of Pacific paradise. A certain Friedrich Ritter, an eccentric German doctor with a love of nudism, was so enchanted that in 1929 he set off for Floreana with his lover, Dora Strauch, a former patient crippled by multiple sclerosis. Not a man to do things by halves, he foresaw a problem with the lack of dental facilities on the islands, and removed all his teeth before traveling, replacing them with metal dentures.

The couple arrived in Floreana and lived a quiet, nude life of gardening. When Ritter sent dispatches of their experiences back to Germany, however, others inevitably thought it would be a good idea to join them. Visitors came and went, but most were deterred by the challenges of setting up life on such a remote island. The Wittmer family was different, though-father Heinz, pregnant wife Margaret, and their sickly 12-year-old son Harry arrived in 1932. Margaret wrote of the "Herculean task" that confronted them in building a life on Floreana, and their second son Rolf was born in a cave, the first recorded birth in the archipelago. Ritter, however, infamously unsociable and misogynist, was none too pleased at the new arrivals and steadfastly refused to help them, keeping his food supplies to himself.

Shortly afterward, an Austrian woman in her early 40s stepped off a boat wearing riding breeches and carrying a pearl-handled revolver. She called herself Baroness Eloise Wagner von Bosquet and was accompanied by two men—Robert Philipson, whom she referred to initially as her husband, and her lover Rudolf Lorenz. As soon as she arrived, the baroness began causing trouble. She seemed to regard the island as her own and began rifling through the post and supplies, taking what she liked. She bathed naked in the island's only drinking water supply and began charging the other islanders for supplies that she had ordered. The baroness also made no secret of her desire to open a luxury hotel on Floreana and charmed the governor of the islands into giving her 10 square kilometers of land for the construction. United by their dislike of the baroness, Dr. Ritter and the Wittmer family developed closer contacts, and Ritter made formal complaints about her to the Ecuadorian government, but to no avail. By this time, the residents on the islands were well known to the world's media, and luxury yachts began stopping off to see what all the fuss was about.

Meanwhile, the love triangle started to go pear-shaped. Lorenz, initially the baroness's favorite, was jilted and demoted to servant, and the baroness took up with Philipson while eagerly pursuing other men who visited Floreana. Lorenz, humiliated by his treatment and bearing scars from beatings, told residents that the Baroness's title was bogus, her marriage a sham and that she had previously worked as a nightclub dancer and even a spy.

Events took a turn for the worse in March 1934 when the island experienced a severe drought. The baroness announced abruptly that she was leaving for Tahiti with Philipson, as if it were a day trip rather than a 5,000-kilometer voyage. No boat was sighted and nobody saw her leave the island, but she was never seen again. Dora Strauch later recalled hearing a blood-curdling scream in the middle of the night. Lorenz's behavior became increasingly erratic after the baroness' disappearance, while Dr. Ritter seemed strangely calm.

To this day, what happened to the Baroness remains a mystery. If she was indeed murdered, Lorenz is generally agreed to be the prime suspect, while Dr. Ritter didn't entirely escape suspicion. Neither of them lasted long enough to defend themselves, though: In July Lorenz finally raised enough money to take a boat to San Cristóbal with a Norwegian captain named Nuggerud, but they never made it. Four months later their bodies washed up

on remote Marchena in the north, and evidence suggested that they had starved to death. Ritter's demise in November 1934 was equally mysterious. According to Dora Strauch, she accidentally poisoned their chickens with pork meat. Not wanting to waste the chicken meat, she killed them and boiled them, thinking that this would destroy the poison. Despite being a vegetarian, Ritter apparently ate it and fell gravely ill from food poisoning. He died a few days later, allegedly cursing his lover with his dying breath.

Dora Strauch returned to Germany and wrote a book titled *Satan Came to Eden*. She died in 1942. The Wittmers continued to live on the island, Margaret's son Rolf opened a successful tour company, and later the family opened a small hotel, both of which still operate today. Margaret wrote a book that included the events of the 1930s titled *Floreana: A Woman's Pilgrimage to the Galápagos*. She lived to age 95, dying in 2000.

Whether Hollywood will wake up to Floreana's remarkable story of death and intrigue remains to be seen.

THE LATE 20TH CENTURY

Conservation efforts increased in the mid-20th century, and after some islands had been delegated as wildlife sanctuaries in the 1930s, the whole archipelago became a national park in 1959. The Charles Darwin Research Center opened in Puerto Ayora in 1964, followed four years later by the Galápagos National Park Service. This was the start of an effort to study and conserve the islands' unique natural heritage, but it also coincided with an increase in tourism. Ecuadorian company Metropolitan Touring began operating exclusive tours in the 1960s and remains the largest operator in the islands. Scheduled flights began in the early 1970s, and tourism grew rapidly.

As word spread of fortunes to be made from fishing and tourism, immigration to the islands from the mainland gathered pace and led to increasing friction between conservationists, who wanted a minimal human population, and immigrants, who wanted to make a decent living. In 1978 the archipelago was among the first 12 regions in the world to receive UNESCO protection. In 1986 the Galápagos Marine Resources Reserve was created to protect the waters around the islands. Reserve officials then banned unrestricted fishing in the local waters, sparking angry protests that culminated in a group of machete-wielding fishermen seizing the Darwin Center and threatening the life of tortoise Lonesome George. The Ecuadorian government backtracked and reopened the waters around the archipelago to limited commercial fishing in 1995.

By the late 1990s, the effect of introduced species had become painfully apparent to conservationists, and the Ecuadorian government finally responded by passing laws in 1998 aimed at conserving the islands' biodiversity while encouraging sustainable development. An eradication and quarantine program was set up, restrictions on illegal fishing expanded, and the percentage of tourist revenue going to the park itself increased. In 2001, UNESCO designated 133,000 square kilometers of marine reserve around the islands as a World Heritage Site, a move aimed to further protect marine life. That same year, an ecological disaster was narrowly averted when the oil tanker *Jessica* ran aground on San Cristóbal, but favorable winds took most of the fuel away from the islands.

Passing laws is all very well, but if the rules are not respected or enforced effectively, they become useless. Even with tighter regulations, the environmental situation deteriorated after 2001: The lucrative illegal fishing of shark fins and sea cucumbers spiraled out of control, and the local population rose quickly, with locals breeding almost as quickly as the goats they'd introduced. Visitors played a significant role in the problem as well-a tourism boom saw visitor

numbers triple in 15 years to reach 160,000 annually in 2007. The tourism boom was accompanied by a local population boom. Legal residents doubled from 9,000 in 1990 to more than 18,000 in 2001, supplemented by thousands of illegal immigrants.

In 2007 the islands were placed on the UNESCO List of World Heritage in Danger. This widely publicized move seemed to focus minds locally, and Ecuadorian president Rafael Correa's government introduced a series of emergency measures to improve the environmental situation.

The first problem was illegal immigrants. Several thousand people who could not produce the correct paperwork were deported back to the mainland. Furthermore, getting permission to live on the Galápagos is now far more difficult than it used to be. However, this action may be inadequate because a big factor in the growing population is a baby boom. Children on the Galápagos make up nearly half the population, and automatic residency to those born on the archipelago seems to encourage residents to have more children. In 2010 the population of the islands stands at 25,000, still a big increase from the previous census in 2001 in spite of the deportations. The authorities estimate that the legal population is growing at more than 5 percent per year.

As well as the local population, visitor numbers have also spiraled out of control. Tourist arrivals were restricted, and they fell for the first time to 145,000 in 2009, although they rose again to 173,000 in 2010. The costs of tours have increased, but without tougher limits, it seems unlikely that visitor numbers will fall and may even continue to rise.

To tackle illegal fishing, satellite technology has been introduced by the Ecuadorian navy, and people working in fishing have been given assistance to set up lucrative sportfishing tours, where they catch a handful of fish daily rather than box-loads.

The problem of air pollution from fossil fuels is also being addressed. There are ambitious plans to convert the islands to 100 percent renewable energy by 2017—San Cristóbal already receives more than half its energy from this scheme.

After all this action, the Ecuadorian government successfully lobbied to have the islands removed from the UNESCO's danger list in July 2010, a decision welcomed by the travel industry but heavily criticized by scientists and conservationists, who claimed it was premature to judge that the islands are out of danger. One comforting fact for environmentalists is that despite the tourism boom, the 70 visitor sites that they frequent represent only 0.01 percent of the archipelago's total land mass, with the rest of the archipelago out of bounds.

Government and Economy

GOVERNMENT

Democracy in Ecuador has been in place since the end of military rule in 1979. However, the military is never far from the political arena, and military-backed coups have removed several presidents, including Jamil Mahuad in 2000 and Lucio Gutiérrez in 2005, while current president Rafael Correa was kept in power and rescued by his own military in 2010.

Correa has reduced political instability by forming a new political party, Alianza PAIS, which now dominates the national assembly. He has increased presidential powers and, most importantly, followed through every election pledge he made in his first election win. The National Assembly of Ecuador replaced the National Congress in 2009 following the approval of the new constitution. It has 124 seats filled by national and provincial deputies who serve four-year terms.

The regional voting system gives less populated provinces, such as those in the Oriente region and the Galápagos, disproportionate representation, since each deputy needs fewer votes to be elected. The Galápagos are among the 24 *provincias* (provinces), each ruled by a governor. The capital is Baquerizo Moreno on San Cristóbal, even though Puerto Ayora is considerably larger. The local government's focus on economic expansion has frequently come into conflict with the Galápagos National Park and Charles Darwin Research Station. Since 2007, however, when the islands were placed on UNESCO's danger list, most meaningful political decisions have come straight from Correa's left-wing government in Quito. Environmental protection figured prominently in Correa's election manifesto, and tighter regulations on fishing and immigration as well as widespread efforts to eliminate invasive species have been implemented quickly.

ECONOMY

Ecuador's economy balances between relatively small agricultural enterprises, businesses in the Sierra, and huge export projects along the coast. Oil supplies half the country's export earnings, and bananas, cut flowers, shrimp, coffee, and chocolate are the other main exports. After the economic crisis a decade ago, when the national currency, the sucre, was replaced by the U.S. dollar, the Ecuadorian economy has recovered well, posting annual growth of 5 percent 2002-2006, peaking at 7 percent because of high oil prices in 2007, and growth remains high.

On the Galápagos, the main industries are tourism and fishing. Tourism has boomed recently, with tourist arrivals tripling over the past 20 years and the industry generates more than $400 million. However, most of this income has not stayed on the islands, with profits taken instead by tour operators based on the mainland or abroad. The government has recently introduced measures requiring more profits to remain on the islands, and most employees have to be local residents with contracts only granted to nonresidents if the employer can prove that they bring special expertise not available on the archipelago.

The fishing industry has been particularly damaging to the local ecosystem with overfishing and illegal fishing of sharks and sea cucumbers in particular. Many of those working in fishing have been persuaded to move into tourism, and sportfishing has developed as a less damaging pastime.

People and Culture

POPULATION

Ecuador's population currently stands at 15 million and is growing at a rate of about 1 percent per year. Large families are still considered normal, not least because the predominant Roman Catholic religion frowns on birth control. Women still tend to marry young and have children quickly. The effect of this is a very young population—35 percent are under 15, while only 4.5 percent are over 65.

The population has boomed in recent years alongside the tourism boom, rising from under 10,000 in 1990 to over 30,000 in 2007. Most residents originate on the coast and the sierra, with Quito, Guayaquil, and Loja particularly well represented. More than 5,000 of the residents were estimated to be in the archipelago illegally, and several thousand have been deported back to the mainland since 2007. The current population stands at 25,000, and tougher new residency laws have slowed immigration, but another key problem is a baby boom on the archipelago. Babies born here have automatic residency status, and recent estimates put the youth population at nearly 50 percent, a population time bomb that surely cannot be sustainable.

RACIAL GROUPS

The largest racial group is mestizo—people of mixed Spanish and indigenous heritage—although you'll rarely hear anyone refer to themselves by this word. They make up 65 percent of the population. Indigenous people make up 25 percent, mainly living in the mountains. White people of Hispanic descent dominate Ecuador's rich classes (5-7 percent). A small Afro-Ecuadorian population, concentrated mainly in Esmeraldas, Quito, and Guayaquil makes up 3 percent.

On the Galápagos, the vast majority of the population—more than 80 percent—are mestizo, with a relatively small number of indigenous Ecuadorian people (8 percent) compared with mainland Ecuador, probably because most indigenous groups inhabit mountainous or rainforest regions and are not attracted to the Galápagos.

EDUCATION

The level of education on the archipelago is slightly higher than in the rest of Ecuador, with more than 40 percent of the population high school graduates, and 15 percent have university education. There is a branch of Quito's Universidad Central in Puerto Ayora and Universidad San Francisco in Baquerizo Moreno.

ESSENTIALS

Getting There and Around

GETTING AROUND
By Air

The Galápagos can only be reached by flying into either of Ecuador's two international airports, located in Quito and Guayaquil. Tracking down the cheapest fare is more problematic than finding a flight in the first place.

TO AND FROM THE UNITED STATES

American Airlines (U.S. tel. 800/433-7300, tel. 2/226-0900 in Quito, www.aa.com) has daily flights to Ecuador from most major U.S. cities via Miami or New York. **United** (tel. 800/222-333, www.united.com) shuttles its planes through Houston and New York, and some stop in Panama. **Delta** (tel. 800/101-060, www.delta.com) has daily flights from its Atlanta hub. All these airlines can bring you to either Quito or Guayaquil. Newer routes are offered by **Copa** (www.copaair.com) through Panama and by **Lacsa/TACA** (www.taca.com) through Costa Rica. **AeroGal** (www.aerogal.com.ec) and **LAN** (www.lan.com) are competing with new flights from Miami. The trip takes about four hours from Miami and five hours from Houston and Atlanta. Airfares vary

© MICHAEL ZYSMAN

© CAROLINA WESTWOOD

the airport in Baltra

greatly, so shop around; generally you can expect to pay $500-800 for a round-trip ticket.

TO AND FROM CANADA
Most flights from Canada connect through gateway cities in the United States. Air Canada and American Airlines fly from Toronto and Montreal via New York and Miami to Quito. **Travel Cuts** (www.travelcuts.com) is Canada's discount student travel agency, with more than 60 offices throughout the country.

TO AND FROM EUROPE
Of the major European carriers, only **KLM** (www.klm.com) and **Iberia** (www.iberia.com) fly their own planes to Ecuador. KLM goes from Amsterdam and Iberia from Madrid. **Air Comet** and **Air Europa** are new competition from Europe. Other carriers make connections in Caracas, Bogotá, Miami, or New York. Flights take 15-17 hours and airfares vary widely, from $1,000 upward.

A competitive discount travel market in the United Kingdom keeps prices reasonable. **Journey Latin America** (12-13 Healthfield Terrace, Chiswick, London W4 4JE, UK tel. 20/8747-3108, UK fax 20/8742-1312, www.journeylatinamerica.co.uk) and **Trailfinders** (63 Conduit St., London W1S 2GB, www.trailfinders.com) are both recommended.

TO AND FROM AUSTRALIA
AND NEW ZEALAND
There are no direct flights to Ecuador from Australia and New Zealand. The best routes are on Qantas via Los Angeles and Miami, Qantas/LAN via Santiago, or Aerolíneas Argentinas via Buenos Aires. Travel times are a minimum of 24 hours and cost about A$2,000.

TO AND FROM LATIN AMERICA
Although major airlines connect Quito and Guayaquil with most other capitals in South America, it's usually cheapest to cross borders

by bus because international flights are highly taxed. South American airlines include: **Aerolíneas Argentinas** (Argentina), **Lloyd Aéreo Boliviano** (Bolivia), **Gol** and **Varig** (Brazil), **LAN** (Chile), **Avianca** and **TAME Calí** (Colombia), **LAN Perú** and **Nuevo Continente** (Peru), and **SBA** (Venezuela).

Airlines that offer flights within Central America and the Caribbean include **Lacsa/ TACA** in Costa Rica, **Cubana** in Cuba, and **Copa** in Panama. The least expensive air route between Central and South America is via Colombia's tiny Caribbean island of San Andrés, connecting to Cartagena and beyond.

TO THE GALÁPAGOS

Flights to the Galápagos are usually paid separately, although agents can arrange them for you. **TAME** (Quito tel. 2/397-7100, Guayaquil tel. 4/231-0305), **AeroGal** (Quito tel. 2/294-2800, Guayaquil tel. 4/231-0346), and **LAN** (tel. 800/101-075, www.lan.com) all offer round-trip flights to San Cristóbal and Baltra. Prices for foreigners are usually $350-400 from Guayaquil and $400-450 from Quito, although there are occasionally promotional fares. *Censo* (foreign-resident ID) holders pay less, about $260-300, and for local Galápagos residents it's less than $150. Check-in is at least 90 minutes before departure. The flight takes about three hours from Quito, and you're allowed to bring one main piece of luggage up to 20 kilograms. All flights originate in Quito and stop in Guayaquil for at least one hour, where passengers usually disembark while the plane is refueled. Tours should reconfirm flights for you both ways, but if you booked independently, do this yourself. Independent travelers must also make sure they fly to the correct island at the correct time to begin the tour, and arrange this *before* booking the tour.

The **National Park entrance fee** is $100 per person for foreigners and a measly $6 for locals. It's payable in cash only upon arrival at the Galápagos airport. The new **migratory control card** costs $10 and is for both Ecuadorians and visitors. Be sure to keep both the receipt for the fee and the control card—if you lose them, you may have to pay again.

If you're arriving in the Galápagos on an organized tour, you won't have to worry about transfers because you'll be met at the airport by guides who will take you to your hotel or yacht. For independent travelers, it depends which island you arrive on. San Cristóbal is very easy because the airport is very close to the main port, Baquerizo Moreno. You can walk it in 20 minutes, but most people take a taxi ($2). For Santa Cruz, it's more complicated. Flights arrive on the tiny island of Baltra, just north of Santa Cruz. Reaching the main port of Puerto Ayora is a three-stage process. First, take a free 10-minute bus ride south, followed by a 10-minute ferry crossing ($0.80), and then either wait for a bus ($2.50) or take a taxi directly to the port (45 minutes, $15). The entire journey from the airport takes over an hour, although you'll likely be too excited to complain. To return to the airport from Puerto Ayora, take a taxi to the bus terminal north of town, but note that the last bus usually leaves at 9:30 A.M., after which a taxi or private transfer is the only option.

LEAVING ECUADOR

A $44 **exit tax** is levied at Mariscal Sucre International Airport in Quito; leaving from Guayaquil costs $28. The current **duty-free** allowance includes one liter of alcohol, 200 cigarettes or 50 cigars, and a "reasonable quantity" of perfume and gifts totaling no more than $200.

GETTING AROUND

Getting around the Galápagos is easier than it used to be. If you have booked a tour, you don't need to worry about this because all transfers, shuttles, and cruises are prearranged.

By Boat

Traveling between islands is easier nowadays, with daily services on small launches connecting Santa Cruz with San Cristóbal and Isabela. All routes cost $25 per person one-way and take about two hours (2.5 hours for Isabela). There is only one service per day: The ferries leave Isabela at 6 A.M. and San Cristóbal at 7 A.M. and depart Puerto Ayora for both islands at 2 P.M. If numbers are large enough, two boats run; they can get booked up, so reserve one day in advance. There are kiosks on the dock in Puerto Ayora and Baquerizo Moreno. On Isabela, book with a tour operator in the center of Puerto Villamil. It can be a bumpy ride, particularly in the afternoon, so don't eat a big meal beforehand.

By Bus

Bus services are very limited on the islands. The bus service on Santa Cruz runs between Puerto Ayora and the ferry jetty at the far north of the island to get to and from the airport. These services only run from the port in the early morning until 9:30 A.M., and return to the port mid-morning until around lunchtime, when the flights arrive. You could hop on one of these buses into the highlands. On San Cristóbal, there are several buses per day into the highlands from Baquerizo Moreno to Progreso.

Interisland Flights

If you're in a hurry and can spare the extra cost, take an interisland flight with **Emetebe,** which has an office on Santa Cruz (Los Colonos and Darwin, top Fl., Puerto Ayora, tel. 5/252-6177). Small eight-seat planes fly half-hour routes among San Cristóbal, Baltra, and Isabela several times per week. Airfares start at $160 one-way, $260 round-trip. **TAME** (tel. 5/252-6527) has an office in Puerto Ayora at Darwin and 12 de Febrero, as does **AeroGal** (Rodríguez Lara and San Cristóbal, tel. 5/244-1950). In Baquerizo Moreno, book at the airport. On Isabela, Emetebe has a small office just off Puerto Villamil's central plaza.

Camionetas and Taxis

In each of the three main ports, white *camionetas* (pickup trucks) are available for hire, and most destinations in town cost $1. Trips into the highlands by taxi cost from $30 for a half day, $50 for a full day.

Walking and Biking

It's better for the environment to vote with your feet and either walk or rent a bike ($15 per day or $3 per hour, deposit usually required) rather than taking a taxi *camioneta*. Some higher-end hotels offer free use of bicycles.

Gateway Cities

QUITO

Ecuador's capital is a city that scales many heights, not least in terms of altitude. The second-highest capital in the world after Bolivia's La Paz, Quito (population 1.8 million) sits at 2,850 meters above sea level in a valley hemmed in by mountains, including the twin peaks of Volcán Pichincha. Quito's dramatic geographical position gives the city a long, thin shape: spread out over 50 kilometers long, but just 8 kilometers wide.

Quito is best-known for the wealth of colonial architecture in the Old Town: churches, monasteries, and museums set among stately plazas and cobbled streets. The city also has several breathtaking viewpoints to appreciate its dramatic location. The New Town is quite a contrast, with plenty of international restaurants, hotels, and tourism services, but it also has some interesting museums. Note that Quito's altitude can leave you feeling breathless and light-headed, so take things slowly, eat light food, avoid alcohol, and take a rest if you feel dizzy.

Airport

The **Mariscal Sucre International Airport** (UIO, tel. 2/294-4900, www.quiport.com) is due to move in 2012 from the intersection of 10 de Agosto, Amazonas, and De la Prensa to the town of El Quinche, 18 kilometers east of the city. This new terminal, costing over $500 million, will host all national and international flights on a 1,500-hectare site and will accommodate over five million passengers per year. When it opens, getting to Quito will take quite a bit longer—a minimum of 45 minutes. There will be shuttle services to the Old and New Town, but details are unconfirmed at the time of writing. A taxi is likely to set you back $15.

Until the new airport opens, it's straightforward getting to and from the old Mariscal Sucre airport. A taxi ride is your best bet—about $3 to the New Town, $5 to the Old Town, but to get these prices you need to flag down a cab outside the terminal car park; otherwise add a couple of dollars to the prices. Buses marked "Aeropuerto" head down 9 de Octubre, 12 de Octubre, and Juan León Mera, and you can also take the trolley along 10 de Agosto and then transfer onto the Rumiñahui connecting bus *(alimentador)* from the Estación Norte, or onto the Metrobus on América, which stops at the airport. However, be wary of pickpockets on these services. From the airport, take pretty much any bus heading south (left) to reach both New and Old Town.

Services at the airport include visitor information, a post office, late-night money exchange, duty-free shops, phone company Andinatel, and a few restaurants and cafés.

Getting Around

The easiest way to get around are the three main electric bus routes running north to south. All charge a flat fare ($0.25) and run every 10 minutes 6 A.M.-11 P.M. daily with shuttle services between the train stations during the night. El Trole runs from Estación Norte down 10 de Agosto to the Old Town and farther south to El Quitumbe terminal. It returns north on Flores and Montufar. Ecovía runs mainly along 6 de Diciembre from Río Coca in the north to Plaza la Marín in the Old Town. Metrobus runs from Carcelén and Ofelia bus stations in the north down América to Universidad Central. However, note that the biggest problem when using bus services in Quito is **pickpocketing.** If you are sightseeing, carrying cameras and valuables, *do not* use these services; take a prearranged taxi instead.

Taxis are good value in Quito and are recommended at night. Most taxis use a meter. Fares should be no more than $2-3 from the Old Town to the New Town. Crime can also be a problem in taxis, so the safest option is to ask your hotel manager to recommend a company and prebook it for you. If you hail a yellow cab, make sure it has a registered taxi number on the side of the car and on the windshield, and that the driver has official ID.

Sights and Tours

If the altitude doesn't make your head spin, the amount to see in Quito probably will. If you only have a couple of days here, spend one each in Old Town and New Town.

In the **Old Town,** start at the 16th-century square **Plaza Grande** and take in the **cathedral.** Visits are available through the museum (Venezuela, tel. 2/257-0371, 9:30 A.M.-4 P.M. Mon.-Sat., $1.50). There's a collection of 17th-18th-century religious art, the tomb of liberator Mariscal Sucre, and a memorial to conservative president Gabriel García Moreno. The **Palacio Presidencial** (10 A.M.-5 P.M.

Tues.-Sun., free) is worth visiting for the guided tours of the impressive interior. Half a block to the south is **La Compañía** (9:30 A.M.-5 P.M. Mon.-Fri., 9:30 A.M.-4 P.M. Sat., 1:30-4 P.M. Sun., $3), one of the most beautiful churches in the Americas and certainly the most extravagant. Seven tons of gold supposedly ended up on the ceiling, walls, and altars of "Quito's Sistine Chapel," built by the wealthy Jesuit order between 1605 and 1765. Turn right and walk west up to the **Plaza San Francisco,** one of Ecuador's most beautiful squares, dominated by the church and monastery of the same name (8 A.M.-noon and 3-6 P.M. daily). It's the oldest colonial edifice in the city and the largest religious complex in South America. To the right of the main entrance, the **Museo Fray Pedro Gocial** (tel. 2/295-2911, 9 A.M.-5:30 P.M. Mon.-Sat., 9 A.M.-12:30 P.M. Sun., $2) houses one of the finest collections of colonial art in Quito.

One of the best places to enjoy Quito's spectacular setting is **La Basílica** (9 A.M.-5 P.M. daily, $2). Walk eight blocks northeast from Plaza Grande on Venezuela. Take an elevator up to take in the fantastic but unnerving views. Another spectacular view over the city is from **El Panecillo,** a 30-meter statue of the Virgin of Quito on the hill at the south end of the city. The close-up view of the Virgin with a chained dragon at her feet is equally impressive. You can climb up inside the base (9 A.M.-5 P.M. Mon.-Sat., 9 A.M.-6 P.M. Sun., $1) to an observation platform. Note that the neighborhood on the way up is dangerous, so take a taxi and ask the driver to wait. A taxi ride costs about $3-4 one-way, $8 round-trip with a short wait.

In the New Town, don't miss the **Museo del Banco Central** (tel. 2/222-3392, www.cce.org. ec, 9 A.M.-5 P.M. Tues.-Fri., 10 A.M.-4 P.M. Sat.-Sun., $2), arguably Ecuador's best museum, with an enormous collection of pre-Columbian ceramics and artifacts as well as colonial,

President Rafael Correa has opened up the Palacio Presidencial to the public.

republican, and modern art. The museum is divided into four rooms: archaeology, colonial art, contemporary art, and the Gold Room, which displays the majestic Inca sun mask, the symbol of the museum.

Another highlight of the New Town is the **Guayasamín Museum** (Bosmediano 543, tel. 2/244-6455, 10 A.M.-5 P.M. Mon.-Fri., $3). Pre-Columbian figurines and pottery fill the first building, while Guayasamín's paintings and an impressive collection of colonial art wait farther on. Even more impressive is **Capilla del Hombre** (Calvachi and Chávez, tel. 2/244-8492, www.capilladelhombre.com, 10 A.M.-5:30 P.M. Tues.-Sun., $3), dedicated to the struggles of indigenous people. Huge paintings fill the open two-story building, centered on a circular space beneath an unfinished dome mural portraying millions of workers who died in the silver mines of Potosí, Bolivia. Take a taxi for about $2 from the New Town or take a "Bellavista" bus from Parque Carolina.

Outside Quito, you may have time to take the **TelefériQo** cable car ride (tel. 2/225-0825, 10 A.M.-7 P.M. Sun.-Thurs., 10 A.M.-10 P.M. Fri.-Sat., $4), which climbs the slopes of Volcán Pichincha to 4,000 meters. TelefériQo shuttles run from Río Coca and 6 Diciembre (Ecovia) and Estación Norte (Trole).

Another enjoyable trip is to **La Mitad del Mundo** (Middle of the World) tourism complex (tel. 2/239-5637, 9 A.M.-6 P.M. Mon.-Fri., 9 A.M.-8 P.M. Sat.-Sun., www.mitaddelmundo.com, $3), 14 kilometers north of the city. The centerpiece is a 30-meter-high monument topped by a huge brass globe; a bright red line bisecting it provides the backdrop for the obligatory photo op. To get here, take the Metrobus on Avenida América to the Ofelia terminal and catch the connecting "Mitad del Mundo" bus.

The Quito Visitors Bureau works with the Tourism Unit of the Metropolitan Police (tel. 2/257-0786) to provide **guided tours** of the city. These well-informed officers are clad in blue and red uniforms and look rather like airline pilots. Tours of the Old Town range $6-15 per person, and a tour of Mitad del Mundo costs $40 per person. Book a tour at the bureau's main office at the Palacio Municipal (Plaza de la Independencia, Venezuela and Espejo, tel. 2/257-2445, www.quito.com.ec, 9 A.M.-6 P.M. Mon.-Fri., 9 A.M.-5 P.M. Sat.).

Accommodations and Food

Most visitors stay in the New Town because there are so many amenities for visitors. However, staying in the Old Town is increasingly possible and offers a more authentic experience.

In the New Town, good budget options with simple guest rooms and a choice of shared and private baths include **The Backpacker's Inn** (Rodríguez E7-48 at Reina Victoria, tel. 2/250-9669, www.backpackersinn.net, $6.50 dorm, $11 s, $16 d), **Hostal New Bask** (Lizardo García and Almagro, tel. 2/256-7153, www.newhostalbask.com, $6 dorm, $16 s or d), **Hostal Blue House** (Pinto and Almagro, tel. 2/222-3480, www.bluehousequito.com, dorm $8-9, $18 s, $24-30 d), and **Loro Verde** (Rodríguez 241 at Almagro, tel. 2/222-6173, www.hostaloroverde.com, $15 s, $28 d, breakfast included). In the midrange, try the more comfortable furnished guest rooms of **Hostal El Arupo** (Rodríguez E7-22 at Reina Victoria, tel. 2/255-7543, $30 s, $45 d), **Fuente de Piedra II** (Mera and Baquedano, tel. 2/290-0323, $56, breakfast included), or **Casa Sol** (Calama 127 at 6 de Diciembre, tel. 2/223-0798, www.lacasasol.com, $48 s, $68 d). At the top end, options include the colonial **Café Cultura** (Robles 513 at Reina Victoria, tel. and fax 2/222-4271, www.cafecultura.com, $100 s, $122 d) or the ultramodern **JW Marriott Hotel Quito** (Orellana 1172 at Amazonas, tel. 2/297-2000, fax 2/297-2050, www.marriott.com, $162 s or d).

In the Old Town, budget choices include the ideally located **Hostal Sucre** (Bolívar 615 at

Cuenca, tel. 2/295-4025, $4-10 pp) on Plaza San Francisco as well as backpacker favorite **Secret Garden** (Antepara E4-60 at Los Ríos, tel. 2/295-6704, www.secretgardenquito.com, dorm $9 pp, room $24-30) farther out of the Old Town. In the midrange are several attractive colonial options. Try the guest rooms around a courtyard at **Hotel San Francisco de Quito** (Sucre 217 at Guayaquil, tel. 2/228-7758, tel. and fax 2/295-1241, www.sanfrancisco-dequito.com.ec, $30 s, $48 d) or recently renovated **Hotel Catedral** (Mejia 638 at Benalcázar, tel. 2/295-5438, www.hotelcatedral.ec, $31 s, $55 d, breakfast included). At the top end, lavish colonial options include **El Relicario del Carmen** (Venezuela and Olmedo, tel. 2/228-9120, www.hotelrelicariodelcarmen.com, $105 s, $135 d) and **Patio Andaluz** (García Moreno and Olmedo, tel. 2/228-0830, www.hotelpatioandaluz.com, $200 s or d).

For restaurants, you are spoiled for choice for international options in the New Town. **The Magic Bean** (Foch 681 at Mera, tel. 2/256-6181) and **Coffee and Toffee** (Calama and Almagro, tel. 2/254-3821, 24 hours daily, entrées $3-6) are both good breakfast options. For Indian try **Chandani Tandoori** (Mera and Cordero, tel. 2/222-1053, noon-10 P.M. Mon.-Sat., noon-5 P.M. Sun., entrées $3-5). For Vietnamese and Thai, try **Uncle Ho's** (Calama and Almagro, tel. 2/511-4030, noon-11 P.M. Mon.-Sat., entrées $5-8), and for Mongolian barbecue, **Mongo's Grill** (Calama E5-10 at Mera, tel. 2/255-6159, noon-11 P.M. Mon.-Sat., entrées $3-8). For pizza, head to **Al Forno** (Moreno and Almagro, tel. 2/252-7145, noon-3 P.M. and 6:30-11 P.M. Mon.-Sat., entrées $6-14), and to treat yourself to Mediterranean specialties, try the colorful, creative atmosphere of **La Boca del Lobo** (Calama 284 at Reina Victoria, tel. 2/254-5500, 5 P.M.-midnight Mon.-Sat.). Ecuadorian options include **Mama Clorinda** (Reina Victoria 1144 at Calama, tel. 2/254-4362, 11 A.M.-10 P.M.

Mon.-Sat.) and **La Choza** (12 de Octubre 1821 at Cordero, tel. 2/223-0839, lunch noon-4 P.M. daily, dinner 7-10 P.M. Mon.-Fri.).

In the Old Town, coffee and snacks are good at **El Cafeto** (Chile and Guayaquil, no phone, 8 A.M.-7:30 P.M. Mon.-Sat., 8 A.M.-noon Sun.) and ice cream is good at **Frutería Monserrate** (Espejo Oe2-12, tel. 2/258-3408, 8 A.M.-7:30 P.M. Mon.-Fri., 9 A.M.-6:30 P.M. Sat.-Sun., $2-5). Good Ecuadorian food and great views are available at **Tianguez** (Plaza San Francisco, tel. 2/295-4326, www.tianguez.org, 10 A.M.-6 P.M. Mon.-Tues., 10 A.M.-11 P.M. Wed.-Sun., entrées $3-5). To treat yourself to a gourmet international meal, head to **Las Cuevas de Luis Candela** (Benalcázar 713 at Chile, tel. 2/228-7710, 10 A.M.-11 P.M. daily, entrées $7-10).

After dinner, there is plenty of **nightlife** in the New Town, centered around Plaza Foch in Mariscal Sucre, but take care at night and always take a taxi back to your hotel. In the Old Town, La Ronda has a selection of pleasant cafés and bars, some offering live music.

Information and Services

The **Corporación Metropolitana de Turismo** (Quito Visitors Bureau) is the best visitor information bureau in Ecuador and an excellent source of information on Quito, with maps, brochures, leaflets, English-speaking staff, and a regularly updated website. The main office is at the Palacio Municipal (Plaza de la Independencia, Venezuela and Espejo, tel. 2/257-2445, www.quito.com.ec, 9 A.M.-6 P.M. Mon.-Fri., 9 A.M.-5 P.M. Sat.). There are also branches in Mariscal (Reina Victoria and Luis Cordero, tel. 2/255-1566), the airport (tel. 2/330-0164), the Museo Nacional del Banco Central (6 de Diciembre and Patria, tel. 2/222-1116), and at Quitumbe bus terminal.

ATMs for most international systems (Plus, Cirrus, Visa, and MasterCard) can be found at major banks along Amazonas and around the shopping centers. These tend to have limits on how much you can withdraw per day (usually $500), so if you need to pay cash for a Galápagos trip, you'll have to go to a bank branch. It's best to take a taxi straight to the travel agency if you're withdrawing a large amount of money, as robberies are a problem in Quito. **Banco del Pacífico** has its head office at Naciones Unidas and Los Shyris, and there is a branch on Amazonas and Washington. **Banco de Guayaquil** is at Reina Victoria and Colón and at Amazonas and Veintimilla; **Banco de Pichincha** is at Amazonas and Pereira as well as on 6 de Diciembre. **Banco Bolivariano** is at Naciones Unidas E6-99.

GUAYAQUIL

While Quito is Ecuador's capital and cultural center, the largest city is actually Guayaquil. As the economic capital, it used to have little to offer tourists, and the heat and smog were reasons enough to stay away, but the city is doing its best to leave behind its bad reputation, and after a major redevelopment of the center, it's definitely worth a visit. The long waterfront walkway, in particular, is not to be missed, and the nightlife is famously raucous.

More international visitors to the Galápagos are now coming through Guayaquil rather than Quito. Although the city does not have the wealth of cultural attractions that the capital has, one advantage is that the climate is similar to the archipelago. It's also closer to the Galápagos, and of course you don't have to deal with altitude sickness as in Quito, although the humidity can be oppressive much of the year.

Airport

Guayaquil's award-winning **José J. Olmedo International Airport** (GYE, De las Américas, tel. 4/216-9000, www.tagsa.aero) is five kilometers north of the city center. It's Ecuador's only international airport besides Quito's and has flights to a range of North American, South American, and some European destinations. The international departure tax is $28 per person, payable in cash. From the airport, a taxi downtown should be $4-5. Never take an unmarked taxi.

Getting Around

The poor traffic situation downtown means that **local buses** ($0.25) are not really worth it. Service is slow and often jam-packed, and pickpockets can be a problem. The **Metrovía** service ($0.25) is cleaner and faster; the line runs south from Hospital Luis Vernaza to La Catedral, the most convenient stop for the downtown sights, and then farther south. It returns north from Biblioteca Municipal to Las Peñas and north to the bus terminal. However, pickpocketing is also a problem on this service.

Taxi drivers in Guayaquil are notorious for driving badly and overcharging foreigners. Few of them use meters, so negotiate the price in advance. It's worth asking in your hotel for the approximate price and then telling the driver, rather than waiting for them to give you an inflated price. As a guide, short journeys around downtown should be about $2, and trips from downtown to the airport, Urdesa, and other northern district $3-4. Never take unmarked taxis, and it's preferable to ask your hotel to call a taxi from a reputable company. If you're staying downtown, most of the main attractions are within walking distance, but taxis are recommended at night.

Sights and Tours

Guayaquil's city center has plenty to keep you busy for a day or two. The three-kilometer riverside promenade **Malecón 2000** is by far the biggest attraction in the city, with historic monuments, modern sculptures, museums, botanical gardens, fountains, bridges, children's play areas, shopping outlets, and restaurants. The cool breezes off the river and the watchful eye of security guards make Malecón the most

Guayaquil's neo-Gothic cathedral was rebuilt in the 1930s after being destroyed in a fire.

relaxing place to spend time in Guayaquil. The best starting point is **La Plaza Cívica** at the end of 9 de Octubre. A highlight is **La Rotonda,** a statue depicting a famous meeting of South America's two most prominent liberators, José de San Martín and Simón Bolívar. Other highlights include the 23-meter **Moorish Clock Tower** and a river cruise on the *Henry Morgan* (afternoon-evening Sun.-Thurs., late-night Fri.-Sat., $5), a replica of the famous Welsh pirate's 17th-century ship. Walk north to the leafy botanical gardens, with welcome shaded areas and a pleasant café. Farther north is the **Museo Guayaquil en La Historia** (tel. 4/256-3078, 10 A.M.-6:30 P.M. daily, $2.50), which tells a fascinating history of the city in 14 dioramas from prehistoric times to the present. The north end of Malecón culminates in the Banco Central's impressive **Museo Antropológico y de Arte Contemporáneo** (MAAC, Malecón and Loja, tel. 4/230-9383, www.museomaac.

com, 10 A.M.-6 P.M. Tues.-Sat., 10 A.M.-4 P.M. Sun., $1.50, Sun. free), which has an exhibition on ancient history, a huge collection of pre-Columbian ceramics, and a modern art exhibition.

The north end of Malecón connects conveniently with the colorful artistic district of **Las Peñas.** This is the oldest neighborhood in Guayaquil and has the largest concentration of colonial architecture. The main draw is the climb up 444 steps past cafés and art galleries. At the top is an open-air museum, **Museo El Fortín del Santa Ana,** which has original cannons and replicas of Spanish galleons. There is also a small chapel and a lighthouse that can be climbed for fabulous views over the city, the Guayas estuary, and Santay Island to the east. As well as climbing the hill, you can also walk around to the right of the steps along the cobbled street of **Numa Pompillo Llona.** At the end of the street, old meets new at **Puerto Santa Ana.** There are several museums, the most interesting of which is **Museo de la Música Popular Guayaquileña Julio Jaramillo** (10 A.M.-1 P.M. and 2-5 P.M. Wed.-Sat., free), dedicated to Guayaquil's most famous musician.

In the city center, don't miss **Parque Bolívar,** better known as "Parque de las Iguanas." It's the perfect prelude to a Galápagos trip, with dozens of urban iguanas lazing around on the grass. Looming high above it is the city's white **cathedral,** rebuilt in the early 20th century after being destroyed by fire. One block southwest is the **Museo Municipal** (Sucre and Chile, 9 A.M.-5 P.M. Tues.-Sat., free) with fossils, sculptures, artwork, and even shrunken heads.

Outside the city, the eight-hectare **Parque Histórico** (Entre Ríos, tel. 4/283-3807, www.parquehistorico.com, 9 A.M.-4:30 P.M. Wed.-Sun., $3, Sun. $4.50) is definitely worth a visit with wildlife, reconstructed haciendas, colonial architecture, and live shows on the weekend. There are buses to Entre Ríos from the terminal, or get a taxi from downtown ($4-5).

The Malecón 2000, an award-winning three-kilometer riverside walkway, is the pride of Guayaquil.

For guided tours, a small fleet of roofless double-decker "Guayaquil Visión" **tourist buses** make the rounds of the Malecón, Las Peñas, and the major parks and plazas. Ninety-minute tours ($5 pp) leave every two hours from the Plaza Calderón at the south end of the Malecón on weekends and holidays. You can buy tickets on board at the three Malecón stops.

Accommodations and Food

Guayaquil has plenty of high-range accommodations catering to businesspeople and luxury travelers, but good budget accommodations are harder to locate. In the center, **Hotel Mar de Plata** (Junín 718 at Boyacá, tel. 4/231-0580, $10 s, $20 d) is clean and a good value. Another budget option with colorful guest rooms is **Hostal Suites Madrid** (Quisquis 305 at Rumichaca, tel. 4/230-7804, $15 s, $25 d). In the midrange, Spanish-style **Hotel Andaluz**

(Junín 842 at Baquerizo Moreno, tel. 4/230-5796 or 4/231-1057, www.hotelandaluz-ec.com, $25 s, $40 d) is the best deal, or try **Hotel Rizzo** (Ballén and Chile, tel. 4/232-5210, $30 s, $40 d) right on Parque Bolívar. Outside the center, good options include **Tangara Guest House** (Sáenz and O'Leary, Ciudadela Bolivariana, Bloque F, Casa 1, tel. 4/228-4445 or 4/228-2828, $45 s, $55 d, breakfast and airport transfers included), and **Iguanazu Hostal** (Ciudadela La Cogra, Km 3.5, Villa 2, tel. 4/220-1143 or 9/986-7968, www.iguanazuhostel.com, dorm $15 pp, $45 s, $55 d).

At the higher end in the center, try **Hotel Las Peñas** (Escobedo 1215 between 9 de Octubre and Vélez, tel. 4/232-3355, www.hlpgye.ec, $54 s, $61 d), and to blow your budget on the best hotel in town, head to the top-quality guest rooms of **Hotel Oro Verde** (9 de Octubre and Moreno, tel. 4/232-7999, fax 4/232-9350, www.oroverdehotels.com, $160 s,

$170 d, buffet breakfast and airport transfers included).

Many of the best restaurants in town are attached to hotels, but look hard enough and there are plenty of good eateries. **Galleta Pecosa** (10 de Agosto and Boyacá, tel. 4/251-8636, 9 A.M.-8 P.M. Mon.-Sat., 9 A.M.-5 P.M. Sun., $1-3) and **La Española** (Junín and Boyacá, tel. 4/230-2694, 8 A.M.-7:30 P.M. Mon.-Sat., 8 A.M.-3 P.M. Sun., $1-3) are both excellent bakeries and ideal for breakfast. For fruit juices and burgers in an imaginative beach setting, head to **Frutabar** (Malecón and Martínez, tel. 4/230-0743, www.fruta-bar.com, 8 A.M.-midnight daily, entrées $4-6). For Ecuadorian specialties, try **Las 3 Canastas** (Vélez and Chile, no phone, breakfast, lunch, and dinner daily, entrées $3-4); **Aroma Café** (Jardínes Botánicos, Malecón, tel. 9/953-7458, lunch and dinner daily, entrées $5-8), in the botanical gardens of Malecón; or **Arthur's** (Llona 127, tel. 4/231-2230, lunch Mon.-Thurs., dinner Mon.-Sat., entrées $6-10), in Las Peñas

overlooking the river. For grilled meats, **La Parillada del Ñato** (Estrada 1219 at Laureles, Urdesa; or Luque and Pichincha downtown, tel. 4/288-3330, lunch and dinner daily, $4-12) is the best in town. To treat yourself, try Oro Verde's trio of gourmet restaurants **El Patio**, **Le Gourmet** and Swiss-style **Le Fondue** (9 de Octubre and Moreno, tel. 4/232-7999, breakfast, lunch, and dinner daily, entrées $10-20).

Information and Services

The **city tourism office** (Ballén and Pichincha, tel. 4/252-4100, www.guayaquil.gov.ec, 9 A.M.-5 P.M. Mon.-Fri.), opposite the Palacio Municipal, stocks more general information about the city and the area. There's also a small visitor information center in a train car north of La Rotonda on Malecón.

Head to Pichincha and Icaza, near Malecón, to find **Banco del Guayaquil** and **Banco Pichincha,** both of which have ATMs and offer credit-card cash advances. **Banco del Pacífico** has an ATM nearby on Icaza and Pichincha.

Visas and Officialdom

Most travelers entering Ecuador are given a stamp in their passport and a stamped **tourist card** (also called a T-3) upon entry. The duration of the visa is 90 days. If you overstay your visa without extending it, you'll have to pay a $200 fine.

To enter Ecuador, all travelers must have a passport valid for more than six months from the date of entry, a return ticket, and "proof of economic means to support yourself during your stay," which is loosely defined and may involve showing a sheaf of traveler's checks to the immigration authority. The latter two requirements are seldom invoked. Hold onto your stamped visa card; you have to turn it in when you leave.

Tourist visas may be extended beyond the original 90 days to a maximum of 180 days.

However, this is at the discretion of the immigration official, and it's not made easier by the fact that you cannot do it in advance but must go to the immigration office the day before your visa expires. Extensions beyond 90 days are handled in Quito at the Ministry of Foreign Relations (Ministerio de Relaciones Exteriores, Carrión E1-76 at 10 de Agosto, Quito, tel. 2/299-3200, www.mmrree.gob.ec, 8:30 A.M.-1:30 P.M. Mon.-Fri.). In Guayaquil, the office is opposite the bus terminal at Avenida Benjamín Rosales. You cannot extend your visa in the Galápagos, so 90 days is the maximum stay without a work permit. This is strictly enforced under tight new regulations.

Other visas are divided into immigrant (10-I to 10-VI) and nonimmigrant (12-I to 12-X). A study visa is 12-V (up to one year), a work visa is 12-VI (very complicated to get and of variable length), a volunteering visa is 12-VII (up to two years), cultural exchange is 12-VIII (often used for teaching, up to one year), business is 12-IX (variable length), and tourism is 12-X (90 days), the last of which you can bolt onto the end of another visa to extend your stay after completing your work or studies. Costs vary from $30 for a tourism visa to $200 for a working visa. To obtain a visa, call the Ecuadorian consulate in your home country to check the requirements.

To enter the Galápagos, you must obtain the mandatory $10 transit control card from your departure airport (either Quito or Guayaquil). This helps to regulate the exact number of visitors. On arrival in the archipelago there is a mandatory $100 national park entrance fee, payable in cash. It's a hefty fee, but it helps to preserve the islands' fragile ecosystem. If you have a student or cultural visa, you should pay $25, while Ecuadorians pay just $6. As in the rest of Ecuador, the maximum stay on the Galápagos is 90 days, although most visitors stay 5-10 days.

Leaving Ecuador

Tourists with 90-day visa cards simply turn them in at the border and get an exit stamp in their passports. Those with longer visas must present their *censo* (foreign-resident ID) and their passports at the airport when leaving.

Customs

The Galápagos has stricter regulations than other destinations because of the fragile ecosystem. All visitors have their luggage inspected at Quito and Guayaquil airport and before boarding shuttle ferry services between islands. There is a long list of items that are prohibited, including plants, flowers, fungi, seeds, animals, soil, and timber. More relevant to visitors are the regulations on food: Coffee beans, dairy products, meat, and especially fruit and vegetables can all pose risks and are often confiscated by bag inspectors. You're safe with packaged drinks and packaged snacks, but otherwise it's best not to bring any food and drink. If you do bring food, help out by taking the trash off the archipelago in your luggage, or at least make sure you use the recycling containers dotted around the towns. If your bag is searched several times during your visit, understand that this is an essential part of environmental protection, as many visitors either unwittingly or, in some cases, deliberately flout regulations.

Accommodations and Food

HOTELS

The range of accommodations on offer in the Galápagos is not nearly as diverse as on the mainland, and you wouldn't expect it to be. However, the number of hotels on the islands has grown rapidly in recent years, causing accompanying problems. Most hotels are in the middle to high-end category, catering to foreign tour groups, but there are a surprising number of budget lodgings. Puerto Ayora on Santa Cruz has by far the largest range, followed by Baquerizo Moreno on San Cristóbal and a limited range in Puerto Villamil on Isabela. Puerto Velasco Ibarra on Floreana has only two hotels. Prices range anything from $30 for a basic double room in a budget hotel in Puerto Ayora to $400 for a room at a top-class luxury hotel such as Hotel Royal Palm. Be aware that prices go up and availability goes down during peak seasons (Christmas-Easter, and to a lesser extent in July-August). Note that the water quality is poor throughout the islands, so never drink from the faucet.

© RAMIRO SALAZAR

the pool at Finch Bay Eco Hotel, Puerto Ayora

CRUISE TOUR ROOMS

Most visitors used to take cruises, but now numbers are split roughly equally between land-based tours and cruises. The quality of boats ranges from barely passable in economy class to better tourist- and tourist superior-class boats. The best vessels are first class or luxury class. Note though that even on first-class boats, small rooms and a certain amount of seasickness cannot be avoided.

FOOD AND DRINK

Ecuador isn't known for gourmet cookery, but perhaps the best food is found on the coast, and many of these specialties are available on the Galápagos. Prices tend to be considerably higher because, aside from freshly caught seafood, most food is flown or shipped in. Look hard enough in the three main ports, however, and you can find two-course set meals for $4-5. If you are on a tight budget, the best way is to seek out favorite local haunts. In Puerto Ayora, the pedestrianized zone along Binford has particularly good value, and many restaurants along Darwin do set meals without advertising, so check out where the locals are eating.

At breakfast (*desayuno*), for $3-5 you can get *tostada* (toast) or fresh *pan* (bread) with *mantequilla* (butter) and *mermelada* (jam), *huevos* (eggs) served *fritos* (fried) or *revueltos* (scrambled), with *café* (coffee) and *jugo* (juice) to wash it down. Some places offer healthier options such as a bowl of fruit, yogurt, and granola. Locals often eat *bolón,* a fried ball of green plantains filled with cheese or bacon.

For lunch and dinner the best food on offer is, of course, seafood. Popular fish include *corvina* (white sea bass) and dorado. Fish is usually offered *frito* (fried), *apanada* (breaded and fried), *al vapor* (steamed), *a la plancha* (filleted and baked, literally "on the board"), or *al ajillo* (in garlic sauce). *Camarones* (shrimp) are also popular, and other shellfish include *cangrejo* (crab), *calamare* (squid), *ostione* (oysters), and *langosta* (lobster or jumbo shrimp). Another popular specialty, originating from the north coast, is *encocado,* seafood cooked with sweet coconut milk. *Patacones,* small pieces of plantain mashed flat and fried crispy, usually accompany seafood dishes and originally hail from Colombia. Salads accompanying seafood tend to come with a dressing made from lemon juice and salt.

Ceviche is one of Ecuador's most famous dishes and consists of seafood (often raw), onions, and coriander marinated in lemon or lime juice, often served with a dish of popcorn on the side. When shrimp is used in ceviche, it's cooked beforehand, but those made with raw *pescado* (fish) or *concha* (clams) may pose a health risk. If you prefer your seafood soup hot, try *sopa de pescado* (fish soup).

Rice and beans are common accompaniments of any meal. Beans are usually cooked in a sauce and served as *menestra,* which can also be made with lentils. Meats include *lomo* (beef, also called *res* or simply *carne,* "meat") and *chancho* (pork), served *a la parilla* (roasted) or *asada* (grilled). *Chuletas* are pork chops, and *hamburguesas* are burgers. A local meat specialty is a *seco,* literally a "dry" stew, but in practice it usually has a sauce made of tomatoes, onions, and coriander. Choose beef, *pollo* (chicken), or *chivo* (goat). *Estofado* is another type of stew made with either chicken or meat and usually containing potatoes and carrots.

Bistec is a version of beefsteak, usually cooked with tomatoes and onions.

If Ecuadorian specialties are not for you, Puerto Ayora has a wide range of international cuisine, including Italian, Chinese, and even sushi. There are also a few good international options in Baquerizo Moreno.

As on the mainland, a vast range of fresh fruit is available, which locals make into *jugos* (juices) and *batidos* (milk shakes). They're often made very sweet, and you can ask for less sugar (*menos azucar*). A juice is usually included with a set meal. Local beers include Pilsner (small or large bottles), weaker Pilsner Light (small bottles) and stronger Club Verde (small bottles and cans), but beer connoisseurs will be disappointed. Go easy on the alcohol, as sailing and a hangover make a horrendous combination.

On the downside, the cleanliness of the water supply in the ports of the Galápagos is poor. Hygiene in very cheap restaurants can be a problem, and food poisoning does happen, although a mild case of diarrhea is more common. In the good hotels and restaurants, you're less likely to be sick. The biggest culprits are unpeeled raw fruit and vegetables, salads, ice, pork, and shellfish. Needless to say, always buy bottled water, and never drink from the faucet. If you do get sick, medicine can be obtained easily from a pharmacy in the port, or your guide may have some available. A stronger case of diarrhea may require antibiotics, worth considering because they tend to work very fast.

Conduct and Customs

Ecuadorians are renowned for their laid-back attitude, which contrasts strongly with North American and European reliance on rules, regulations, and schedules. This relaxed demeanor shows itself in many aspects of life in Ecuador—on the plus side, the people are very friendly, hospitable, and extroverted, while on the downside, they are infamously unpunctual, and the culture as a whole is comparatively disorganized.

The culture on the Galápagos Islands, although still officially Ecuadorian, is more organized than on the mainland. Due to the tight travel schedules, punctuality does tend to be respected. Additionally, the effect of so many international tourists and a permanent scientific community means that many people you meet—but not all—are also more open-minded and educated than on the mainland.

One area where people in the Galápagos are less laid-back is religion. As on the mainland, people are deeply religious, the vast majority Catholic, and evangelical Christianity is rising fast. Note that belief in God is usually assumed, and atheism is considered abnormal, so it's best to avoid too much religious discussion. Ironically, like creationists in North America, many locals believe the world is 6,000 years old and reject the theory of evolution that made the Galápagos famous.

Greetings and General Politeness

Latin Americans are much more physical in day-to-day interactions than their northern neighbors. Men give a firm handshake to other men both when arriving and leaving; women give one or two pecks on the cheek when being introduced to another woman, and usually to another man. These actions aren't usually expected of foreign clients, but a handshake is always appreciated as a greeting or expression of gratitude at the end of a tour. Verbal greetings are essential; *hola* (hello) is often followed by *¿Como está?* (How are you?), even if you don't know the person. It's normal to begin any conversation with *Buenos días/tardes/noches,* and even complete strangers will greet each other this way, unprompted. If you see someone eating, it's polite to say *Buen provecho* (Enjoy your meal), again even to strangers. This use of physical and verbal greetings is all part of the Latin American concern for appearances. It is frowned upon to be rude in public, and foreigners often acquire a reputation for being unfriendly, bordering on rude, if they don't use greetings properly. It's also a quick way to make friends.

Gender and Sexuality

Latin American culture is very polarized. Men tend to be the traditional heads of the household, and women manage the home and raise the children. Recently, though, Latin American women have begun to assert themselves and claim new freedoms in work and daily life. A great enemy of feminism is, of course, machismo, which manifests in ways ranging from subtle to blatant. Whistles and catcalls are seen as harmless, but men find themselves feeling they have to prove their manhood in their posturing, driving, and womanizing. Unfortunately, the Galápagos is no exception to this, and female travelers frequently complain about unwanted attention from crew members and even guides. Make clear that you're not interested, and perhaps regular references to a fiancé (*novio*) and a ring on the appropriate finger would help. Don't be afraid to confront locals about sexism, but bear in mind that making an Ecuadorian look bad in public is not to be treated lightly and will likely lead to resentment.

Machismo extends to attitudes toward gays and lesbians, and even though same-sex civil unions are now permitted in Ecuador, homophobia is still pervasive. Gay travelers need to bear in mind that being open about their sexuality can lead to anything from embarrassment and religious rants to violence. There is a burgeoning gay community in Ecuador, however; Quito has the biggest gay scene, and there are a few gay bars in Guayaquil and Cuenca. Some cruise operators offer gay-friendly tours.

Tips for Travelers

OPPORTUNITIES FOR VOLUNTEERS

Volunteer placements on the Galápagos are highly competitive, and it helps to be a science student or university graduate to secure the best opportunities. Most positions available involve either labor-intensive physical work, teaching, or administration based in one of the main ports, so don't come expecting to track wildlife or analyze coral reefs. The **Charles Darwin Foundation** (6 de Diciembre N36-109 at California, Quito, tel. 2/224-4803, Santa Cruz tel. 5/252-6146, cdrs@fcdarwin.org.ec, www.darwinfoundation.org) offers the best placements in conservation and environmental science. Other organizations to contact include **Ecuador Volunteers** (Mariscal Foch E9-20 at 6 de Diciembre, Quito, tel. 2/223-4708, www.ecuadorvolunteers.org), UK-based **i-to-i** (UK tel. 800/11-1156, www.i-to-i.com) or visit www.goabroad.com, a useful directory of volunteering and teaching posts worldwide, including the Galápagos.

ACCESS FOR TRAVELERS WITH DISABILITIES

Ecuador is not very well-prepared to receive disabled travelers. Wheelchair ramps are rare on buildings and sidewalks, and disabled toilets are rare. International airports and top-class hotels are the few places where disabled travelers can expect reasonable facilities. On the Galápagos, it's even more problematic because many trails are too uneven for wheelchairs, and wet landings are inaccessible. For more information, contact **Mobility International USA** (45 W. Broadway, Suite 202, Eugene, OR 97401, U.S. TTY tel. 514/343-1284, U.S. fax 514/343-6812, www.miusa.org) and the online **Global Access Disabled Traveler Network** (www.globalaccessnews.com).

Travelers with disabilities have a range of options for travel-planning assistance, including the **Information Center for Individuals with Disabilities** (P.O. Box 750119, Arlington Heights, MA 02475, U.S. fax 781/860-0673, www.disability.net) and the **Access-Able Travel Source** (www.access-able.com). Health escorts can be arranged through **Travel Care Companions** (Box 21, Site 9, RR 1, Calahoo, Alberta T0G 0J0, Canada, tel. 780/458-2023 or 888/458-5801, www.travelcarecompanions.com).

WOMEN TRAVELING ALONE

On the mainland, macho whistles and cat-calls can be a constant problem for female travelers. On the Galápagos, the situation is far better. However, young women traveling without a romantic partner should not be surprised to experience unwanted attention from crew members and even guides. Try to make clear politely but firmly that you're not interested. Wearing a ring on the appropriate finger and regular mention of a fiancé may also help.

WHAT TO TAKE

A trip to the Galápagos requires plenty of preparation. While summer clothes are clearly first in the suitcase, there are plenty more items you need to pack. Bring a light jacket or sweater for chilly mornings and cool evenings, plus a rain jacket for visiting the damp highlands. Good walking shoes should be packed along with the flip-flops for negotiating rough lava trails. Most importantly, bring a hat, sunglasses, and plenty of sunblock to protect you from the fierce equatorial sun, which is doubly strong at sea. A refillable water bottle is very useful and also reduces the islands' problem with plastic. Seasickness is a common problem in the Galápagos, both on cruises and particularly on the fast ferries between islands, so bring seasickness pills. Bring a day pack to take on excursions, and don't forget your swimming gear. You can bring your own snorkel if you prefer, although tours usually provide them.

Last but not least, bring a decent camera. The Galápagos is hard to beat for photography, so if you were going to consider upgrading, do it before you visit. Also consider investing in a telephoto lens, bring UV and polarizing filters, and bring a decent bag to protect the equipment from water. Bring far more film or digital memory than you'll think you'll need, and expect to take several hundred photos.

TRAVELING WITH CHILDREN

Children are considered life's greatest reward in Latin America, so parents traveling with children will enjoy compliments and assistance across the continent. However, the Galápagos are certainly a challenging destination to visit with young children. Infants under two usually travel free, but it's hardly recommended. If you are planning to take the whole family, wait until they are old enough to tackle hikes, swimming, and snorkeling. Many Galápagos tour operators offer discounts of around 25 percent for children under age 12, but teenagers tend to pay full price.

GAY AND LESBIAN TRAVELERS

By and large Ecuador still has a homophobic culture, and many gay people are either in the closet or keep their sexuality well-guarded. Things have changed in recent years, however, and the 2008 constitution guarantees civil rights to gays and lesbians and allows same-sex civil unions. Despite this, gay and lesbian travelers are advised to keep a low profile on mainland Ecuador. Quito has the most developed gay scene, with several bars in the New Town, while Cuenca and Guayaquil also have a few bars. On the Galápagos, most tour operators operate gay-friendly cruises. A useful website is www.galapagosgay.com.

SENIOR TRAVELERS

The Galápagos is very popular with senior travelers, and most operators are accustomed to dealing with seniors. However, make sure you can handle the physical demands of the tours—some Galápagos hikes are steep and strenuous, and you need to be a confident swimmer to go snorkeling. Don't be embarrassed to sit out a hike or swimming trip if you feel tired. Bring along a printed medical history and enough prescription medications for the entire trip, plus extra.

AARP (U.S. tel. 888/687-2277, www.aarp.org) offers a Purchase Privilege Program for discounts on airfares, car rentals, and hotels. **Road Scholar** (U.S. tel. 800/454-5768, www.roadscholar.org) is the educational program of Elderhostel, a 35-year-old nonprofit, and offers educational adventures for adults over age 55.

Health and Safety

BEFORE YOU LEAVE

Travelers to tropical (i.e. northern) South America must take a number of specific health concerns into consideration. Major hospitals and those attached to universities in your home country usually have **traveler's clinics** or **occupational medicine clinics** that can recommend and administer pretravel vaccinations. Also check with your local Department of Public Health for an **immunization clinic.** If you're sufficiently informed, you might just be able to walk in with a list of the shots and pills you want.

Note that regulations on dishing out medication are very loose in Ecuador. The upside is that you can walk into a pharmacy and get hold of a range of medicines without a prescription, but the downside is that supplies are often low and you have to be wary of unqualified pharmacists trying to sell you expensive, inappropriate medication. Make sure you know exactly what you're taking before it goes in your mouth (a quick Internet search can help).

To stay healthy, the best you can do while traveling—besides taking any prescriptions you brought along—is to wash your hands often, pay attention to what you eat and drink, and be on the lookout for any unusual symptoms. Buying alcohol-based hand sanitizer is very useful, and a basic first-aid kit is a must. The last thing you'd expect in the Galápagos is to catch a cold or the flu, but these illnesses are very common in Ecuador, even in tropical areas, and the nature of a group tour means that they can be passed on quickly, so take precautions when possible.

Recommended Vaccinations

Vaccinations are recorded on a yellow **International Certificate of Vaccination,** which you should bring with you to Ecuador.

You may be asked to show this document to prove your immunizations, especially in the case of a yellow fever outbreak. Take care of these vaccinations as soon as possible, since some involve a series of injections and take a few months to take effect. Your doctor should know which ones not to mix with others (especially immunoglobulins) so as not to decrease their effectiveness. See your doctor at least 4-6 weeks before you leave to allow time for immunizations to take effect. The following vaccinations are recommended for travelers to Ecuador. Even if you are only spending minimal time on the mainland before traveling to the Galápagos, you should still consider these vaccinations.

Hepatitis A: This viral infection of the liver is contracted mainly from contaminated food and water. The vaccination is strongly recommended, and a booster after 6 or 12 months guarantees protection for over 10 years. Get the first shot before you leave; it's possible to get a follow-up shot from a good private clinic in Ecuador.

Typhoid fever: This dangerous gut infection is also acquired from food and water. The vaccination is strongly recommended and can be administered as a live oral vaccine or through two injections taken at least four weeks apart.

Yellow fever: This vaccination is necessary when entering Ecuador from Peru or Colombia (both officially infected countries), but it's a good idea in any case because it's a dangerous disease.

Hepatitis B: This is a less-common travelers' disease because it's contracted through sexual contact or exposure to infected blood. The vaccination is recommended for longer-term travel (more than six months) and if you are likely to come into close contact with locals (for example, working in medicine). This disease is more insidious than others, and you can be a carrier for years without symptoms, but it can cause serious liver damage. The complication is that you need three vaccinations spaced a month apart.

Routine immunizations: Any trip is a good time to update the following: diphtheria-tetanus, influenza, measles, mumps, poliomyelitis, and pneumococcus.

SUNBURN

The Galápagos straddles the equator, and all those hikes and swims in the equatorial sun, not to the mention the reflection of the sun off the sea, will leave you burned to a crisp if you don't take precautions. Sunscreen (SPF 30 and above), lip balm, and a wide-brimmed hat will help protect you. A good pair of sunglasses with UV protection is also essential.

DISEASES FROM FOOD AND WATER

If you're going to get sick while traveling, it will probably be from contaminated water or food. As a tropical country, Ecuador is full of bacteria and parasites, and the Galápagos is no exception. Get in the habit of washing your hands at least 2-3 times a day, preferably before every meal and certainly after every restroom visit.

Hygiene is generally of a good standard on organized tours, and you're more likely to get sick eating and drinking at cheap places in the ports. Even then, it's less likely than on mainland Ecuador. Obviously, drink only bottled water and never from the faucet. This becomes more complicated when ordering drinks made with water. To minimize the risk, drink bottled fruit juices or sodas, which are readily available in port and on ships. However, you're bound to want to try the freshly made juices and shakes, which can be a risk because they are occasionally mixed with unpurified water. You'll be fine in reputable hotels, but avoid the cheaper joints. Ice cubes are a particular risk, so ask for drinks *sin hielo* (without ice).

Regarding food, the biggest illness culprit is shellfish. In most cases, you should be fine, but consider reducing your consumption of shrimp and other shellfish if you have a delicate stomach.

No one is safe from **traveler's diarrhea,** although most cases are mild. Ease a low-grade case of the runs with Imodium A-D (loperamide) or Pepto-Bismol, but bear in mind that these medicines are often short-term solutions. Drink plenty of water and noncaffeinated fluids like fruit juice and ginger ale. Oral rehydration solutions are very handy, and if you haven't brought any, they're easy to make: One teaspoon of salt and 2-3 tablespoons of sugar or honey in a liter of water will work. More serious cases may require a doctor's appointment and antibiotics. Your guide may be able to recommend a good antibiotic for bacterial infection to get from the pharmacy.

Dengue fever, transmitted by *Aedes* mosquitoes, is present on the Galápagos, although it is rare. There have been outbreaks occasionally on San Cristóbal, but these are confined to urban areas because the mosquitoes live mainly in dirty water. Flu-like symptoms, such as nausea, bad headaches, joint pain, and sudden high fever are often misdiagnosed as other tropical diseases. Severe cases leading to shock syndrome or hemorrhagic fever are rare, but if you have already had dengue fever, a second case can be more dangerous. The only treatments known so far are rest, fluids, and fever-reducing medications. Medical attention is strongly recommended, if only for diagnosis.

ANIMALS

Most of the creatures on the Galápagos are very tame and pose little threat to humans. However, the national park advises you to keep a minimum distance of two meters from any animal. By far the biggest risk comes from sea lions, usually elderly bulls, and you should stay farther than two meters from them. Attacks are rare, but you must take care and avoid getting too close. The bull will usually bark at you as a warning, which is usually enough to scare anyone off. Note that female sea lions with pups can also be aggressive if they feel threatened.

Information and Services

MONEY
Currency
In September 2000, Ecuador officially laid the beleaguered old sucre to rest and replaced it with the **U.S. dollar.** In the short term the devaluation of the sucre and its subsequent replacement was a financial disaster for millions of Ecuadorians, who saw the value of their savings plummet while prices of basic foods rocketed. Once one of the cheapest Latin American countries for traveling, Ecuador is now in the middle of the price range—cheaper than Colombia and considerably cheaper than Brazil and Chile, but more expensive than Bolivia and Peru. The biggest plus for visitors is that there's no need to worry about exchanging money. The Galápagos, however, are more expensive than mainland Ecuador, with prices comparable to the United States.

Crime is low on the Galápagos, but it's still preferable to avoid carrying large amounts of cash. If you've already booked your tour, you should only need enough for drinks, tips, and occasional meals. If you are traveling independently to pick up a last-minute deal, either bring extra cash or use a cash advance on credit cards from an ATM. Carrying the bulk of your money in **traveler's checks,** preferably U.S. dollars, which can be refunded if lost or stolen, is best. Commissions are often 2-5 percent and sometimes depend on the amount exchanged. American Express and Visa traveler's checks are the most widely accepted, but Thomas Cook and Citibank checks also pass. Be sure to keep the serial numbers and the number to call in a separate place just in case your checks are lost or stolen.

Credit cards are accepted in many higher-end shops, hotels, restaurants, and travel agencies, but there is often a surcharge of up to 10 percent. It's generally best to pay with cash whenever possible and save your credit cards for emergencies or ATM use. MasterCard and Visa are the most widely accepted, and card-holders can draw cash advances. American Express, Diner's Club, and Discover are much harder to use.

Automated teller machines (ATMs) are becoming more and more common in Ecuador. Almost all credit cards issuers can now give you a personal identification number (PIN) so you can use the card to withdraw cash advances at ATMs. Ask for a four-digit PIN, since five-digit ones don't work in Ecuador. Machines accept debit cards on the Plus and Cirrus networks, as well as MasterCard and Visa cards that have been assigned a PIN—call your card issuer for information on setting this up. Most ATMs have a daily withdrawal limit of $300-500 at most. There are ATMs and banks in Puerto Ayora and Baquerizo Moreno, but not in Puerto Villamil.

Tipping
It's customary to tip at the end of a cruise. Remember that, although your tour is expensive, in a country as unequal as Ecuador, the big bucks don't filter down to the lowest level; the crew as well as the guide will very much appreciate your tip. Obviously, use your own judgment on how much to give, and your tip should reflect the level of service. Between 5 and 10 percent of the price of the cruise is considered

normal. Tip the guide separately, and use the tip box for the rest of the crew.

COMMUNICATIONS AND MEDIA
Mail

With the arrival of the Internet and email, "snail mail" systems around the world are shrinking in volume and rising in price. You're better off mailing postcards and letters from mainland Ecuador, although the novelty of dropping off something at Post Office Bay on Floreana may be difficult to resist (don't expect it to arrive any time soon, though).

At the regular post office, airmail postcards and letters under 20 grams cost about $1.55 to North and South America, $1.80 to Europe, $2.40 elsewhere. For mail weighing 20-100 grams, you will pay $3.71 to North and South America, $4.29 to Europe, and $5.28 to anywhere else. Don't mail any objects of value, as things go missing quite often from Ecuador's postal system, especially incoming packages. It's better to use a private courier company like DHL or FedEx.

The regular mail service is notoriously unreliable, and packages are routinely opened by customs (ostensibly checking for contraband). The South American Explorers' Quito clubhouse, American Express, and various Spanish schools can receive and hold mail for members.

Telecommunications

Compared to the postal service, the national telephone system functions well under the auspices of the national phone company. It's currently called Andinatel in the Andes and Pacifictel along the coast. National calls (within the Galápagos and mainland Ecuador) are no problem, but international calls may be impossible. Some offices will charge you for calls if the phone rings more than eight times, even if no one answers. Connections to and from the Galápagos are sometimes congested and tenuous at best.

To make long-distance calls within Ecuador, dial a 0 followed by the regional area code and the seven-digit phone number. Drop the 0 within the same region. Cellular phones are everywhere; their numbers begin with 9 or 8, and you can choose between Movistar and Claro (formerly Porta). For directory information, dial 104; for help with national long distance, dial 105; and for international long distance, dial 116 or 117. Numbers beginning with 800 are toll-free.

To call Ecuador from the United States, dial the international access code (011), the country code for Ecuador (593), the regional area code (2-7) or cell phone code (8 or 9), and the seven-digit local number—that's 15 digits in all. The area code for the Galápagos is 5.

Two competing cellular companies, Movistar and Claro (formerly Porta), offer public pay phones, and each system takes its own type of calling card (*tarjeta telefónica*), which you can buy in various denominations just about anywhere. Phones display the amount left on your card; national calls cost about $0.17 per minute.

Internet

Internet access has exploded like a volcano in Ecuador and the Galápagos in recent years. Instantaneous and inexpensive, email *correo electrónico* and Skype makes it easy to keep in touch with friends back home. Most Internet cafés are open 8 A.M.-10 P.M. daily and charge $1 or less per hour. If you plan to use the Internet to stay in touch, you can set up a free email account through services like Hotmail (www.hotmail.com), Yahoo (http://mail.yahoo.com), or Gmail (www.google.com/gmail). Digital photographers can burn images onto CDs for $2-3 at many Internet cafés, or carry a flash drive. However, the Internet service on the Galápagos is often notoriously slow, and Skyping can be problematic.

Newspapers and Magazines

Local publications include national Spanish-language newspapers such as Quito-based *Hoy* and *El Comercio,* Guayaquil-based *El Universo,* and government-owned *El Telégrafo.* These are sporadically available in the main ports on the islands. It's often easier to keep up to date with local and international news online—or, even better, forget about the rest of the world for a few days!

MAPS AND TOURIST INFORMATION

Maps

International Travel Maps (530 W. Broadway, Vancouver, BC V5Z 1E9, Canada, tel. 604/879-3621, fax 604/879-4521, www.itmb.com) has 150 of its own maps and distributes 23,000 more by other publishers. Its 1:700,000 Ecuador map ($13.95) is the best available. In the United States, maps of Ecuador and South America are available from **Maplink** (30 S. La Patera Lane, Unit 5, Santa Barbara, CA 93117, U.S. tel.

805/692-1394, U.S. fax 805/692-6787, www.maplink.com). In Ecuador, the best resource is the **Instituto Geográfico Militar** (Senierges and Paz y Miño, Quito, tel. 2/397-5100, www.igm.gob.ec), near Parque El Ejido in Quito. Otherwise, you can pick up useful city, town, and regional maps at tourism offices across the country.

Dedicated maps of the Galápagos and detailed street maps of the three main ports are available from tourism offices in Puerto Ayora, Baquerizo Moreno, and Puerto Villamil.

WEIGHTS AND MEASURES

Ecuador and the Galápagos use the international metric system; distances are in kilometers. For short urban distances, the word *manzana,* which usually translates as "apple," refers to residential blocks. Food is usually sold in kilograms, although some products are also sold in pounds, and gas is sold by the U.S. gallon. To avoid confusion you can always ask for a fixed monetary quantity, for example $3 of ham, $20 of gas.

RESOURCES

Glossary

abrazo: a platonic hug

adobe: sun-dried mud brick building

aguardiente: sugarcane alcohol

aguas termales: hot springs

almuerzo: lunch

artesanías: handicrafts

barrioías: district, often a poor neighborhood

batidoías: fruit shake

botas de caucho: rubber boots

brujo/a: witch, practitioner of magic

buseta: mini bus

cabaña: cabin

camioneta: truck, often public transport

campesino/a: rural resident

canelazo: hot sweet alcoholic drink made with sugarcane

cangil: popcorn

caramba: mild expression of surprise

¡carajo!: stronger expression of frustration, mildly offensive

centro comercial: mall

chicha: fermented maize drink

chifa: Chinese restaurant

chifles: chips made with crispy fried plantains

chiva: open-top bus used for parties

cholo: originally coastal fishermen, but also applied as a derogatory term for lower-class uneducated people

choza: thatched hut, sometimes converted into tourist accommodations

colectivo: public bus or truck

cordillera: mountain range

costeño: person from the coast

criollo: originally a person of Spanish descent born in the colonies but now applied to anything traditional, especially food

curandero/a: medicinal healer

cuy: roasted guinea pig

ejecutivo: executive or first class, particularly on buses

fanesca: a fish stew dish served during Lent

finca: small farm

¡fuchi!: exclamation indicating a bad smell

gringo: term for North American, but applied to most white foreigners; not particularly derogatory

guácala: exclamation indicating that you don't like something, most commonly food

hacienda: farm or country estate

helado: ice cream; *helados de paila* is a type of sherbet, an Ecuadorian specialty

hostería: inn

indígena: indigenous person; note that *indio* is considered insulting

invierno: winter or rainy season (relatively hot and wet)

lancha: small boat

lavandería: launderette

lavaseca: dry cleaner

maíz: corn

malecón: riverside or seaside promenade

menestra: lentils or beans cooked in sauce as accompaniment to rice

menú del día: set menu of the day

merienda: supper, also used for cheap set-menu dinners

mestizo: person of mixed indigenous and European blood

minga: community voluntary work

monos: monkeys, a slightly derogatory term used for people from Guayaquil

mosquitero: hanging mosquito screen for beds

municipio: town or city hall

obraje: textile workshop

panadería: bakery

panga: small boat

páramo: high-altitude grasslands

parrillada: restaurant specializing in grilled meat

paseo: stroll or walk, often in the evening

pasillo: Ecuador's national music

pelucón: literally, bigwig; mildly derogatory expression coined by President Rafael Correa to refer to the rich elite

peña: bar with traditional live music

plata: silver, slang for money

propina: tip

quinta: fine country house

quinua: grain native to the Andes

ranchero: wooden bus with open sides, also known as a *chiva*

salchipapas: french fries topped with chunks of hot dog

salsateca: Latin dance club

selva: rainforest

serrano: person from the sierra or mountains

soroche: altitude sickness

SS HH: sign for public restroom (*servicios higiénicos*)

tambo: a small thatched hut used for emergency shelter in the Andes

tarabita: a small cable car

terminal terrestre: bus terminal

tienda: shop

trole: trolley or electric bus

tzantza: shrunken head

verano: "summer," a drier and cooler season

Spanish Phrasebook

An important barrier to breach if you're in Ecuador and the Galápagos Islands for an extended period is the language, and your adventure will be far more fun if you use a little Spanish. It's really not as difficult as you imagine if you put your mind to it. Ecuadorans, although they may smile at your funny accent, will appreciate your halting efforts to break the ice and transform yourself from a foreigner into a potential friend. It will also empower you to be more in control of your travels.

Spanish commonly uses 30 letters—the familiar English 26, plus four straightforward additions: ch, ll, ñ, and rr, which are explained in "Consonants," below.

PRONUNCIATION

Once you learn them, Spanish pronunciation rules—in contrast to English—don't change. Spanish vowels generally sound softer than in English. (*Note:* The capitalized syllables below receive stronger accents.)

Vowels

a like ah, as in "hah": *agua* AH-gooah (water), *pan* PAHN (bread), and *casa* CAH-sah (house)

e like ay, as in "may:" *mesa* MAY-sah (table), *tela* TAY-lah (cloth), and *de* DAY (of, from)

i like ee, as in "need": *diez* dee-AYZ (ten), *comida* ko-MEE-dah (meal), and *fin* FEEN (end)

o   like oh, as in "go": *peso* PAY-soh (weight), *ocho* OH-choh (eight), and *poco* POH-koh (a bit)

u   like oo, as in "cool": *uno* OO-noh (one), *cuarto* KOOAHR-toh (room), and *usted* oos-TAYD (you); when it follows a "q" the **u** is silent; when it follows an "h" or has an umlaut, it's pronounced like "w"

Consonants

b, d, f, k, l, m, n, p, q, s, t, v, w, x, y, z, and ch pronounced almost as in English; **h** occurs, but is silent—not pronounced at all

c   like k as in "keep": *cuarto* KOOAR-toh (room), Tepic tay-PEEK (capital of Nayarit state); when it precedes "e" or "i," pronounce **c** like s, as in "sit": *cerveza* sayr-VAY-sah (beer), *encima* ayn-SEE-mah (atop)

g   like g as in "gift" when it precedes "a," "o," "u," or a consonant: *gato* GAH-toh (cat), *hago* AH-goh (I do, make); otherwise, pronounce **g** like h as in "hat": *giro* HEE-roh (money order), *gente* HAYN-tay (people)

j   like h, as in "has": *Jueves* HOOAY-vays (Thursday), *mejor* may-HOR (better)

ll   like y as in "yes": *toalla* toh-AH-yah (towel), *ellos* AY-yohs (they, them)

ñ   like ny as in "canyon": *año* AH-nyo (year), *señor* SAY-nyor (Mr., sir)

r   is lightly trilled, with tongue at the roof of your mouth like a very light English d, as in "ready": *pero* PAY-doh (but), *tres* TDAYS (three), *cuatro* KOOAH-tdoh (four)

rr   like a Spanish r, but with much more emphasis and trill. Let your tongue flap. Practice with *burro* (donkey), *carretera* (highway), and Carrillo (proper name), then really let go with *ferrocarril* (railroad)

Note: The single small but common exception to all of the above is the pronunciation of Spanish **y** when it's being used as the Spanish word for "and," as in "Ron y Kathy." In such case, pronounce it like the English ee, as in "keep": Ron "ee" Kathy (Ron and Kathy).

Accent

The rule for accent, the relative stress given to syllables within a given word, is straightforward. If a word ends in a vowel, an n, or an s, accent the next-to-last syllable; if not, accent the last syllable.

Pronounce *gracias* GRAH-seeahs (thank you), *orden* OHR-dayn (order), and *carretera* kah-ray-TAY-rah (highway) with stress on the next-to-last syllable.

Otherwise, accent the last syllable: *venir* vay-NEER (to come), *ferrocarril* fay-roh-cah-REEL (railroad), and *edad* ay-DAHD (age).

Exceptions to the accent rule are always marked with an accent sign: (á, é, í, ó, or ú), such as *teléfono* tay-LAY-foh-noh (telephone), *jabón* hah-BON (soap), and *rápido* RAH-pee-doh (rapid).

BASIC AND COURTEOUS EXPRESSIONS

Most Spanish-speaking people consider formalities important. Whenever approaching anyone for information or some other reason, do not forget the appropriate salutation—good morning, good evening, etc. Standing alone, the greeting *hola* (hello) can sound brusque.

Hello. *Hola.*
Good morning. *Buenos días.*
Good afternoon. *Buenas tardes.*
Good evening. *Buenas noches.*
How are you? *¿Cómo está usted?*
Very well, thank you. *Muy bien, gracias.*
Okay; good. *Bien.*
Not okay; bad. *Mal or feo.*
So-so. *Más o menos.*
And you? *¿Y usted?*
Thank you. *Gracias.*
Thank you very much. *Muchas gracias.*
You're very kind. *Muy amable.*
You're welcome. *De nada.*
Goodbye. *Adios.*
See you later. *Hasta luego.*
please *por favor*

yes *sí*
no *no*
I don't know. *No sé.*
Just a moment, please. *Momentito, por favor.*
Excuse me, please (when you're trying to get attention). *Disculpe* or *Con permiso.*
Excuse me (when you've made a boo-boo). *Lo siento.*
Pleased to meet you. *Mucho gusto.*
How do you say... in Spanish? *¿Cómo se dice... en español?*
What is your name? *¿Cómo se llama usted?*
Do you speak English? *¿Habla usted inglés?*
Is English spoken here? (Does anyone here speak English?) *¿Se habla inglés?*
I don't speak Spanish well. *No hablo bien el español.*
I don't understand. *No entiendo.*
How do you say... in Spanish? *¿Cómo se dice... en español?*
My name is... *Me llamo...*
Would you like... *¿Quisiera usted...*
Let's go to... *Vamos a...*

TERMS OF ADDRESS

When in doubt, use the formal *usted* (you) as a form of address.

I *yo*
you (formal) *usted*
you (familiar) *tu*
he/him *él*
she/her *ella*
we/us *nosotros*
you (plural) *ustedes*
they/them *ellos* (all males or mixed gender); *ellas* (all females)
Mr., sir *señor*
Mrs., madam *señora*
miss, young lady *señorita*
wife *esposa*
husband *esposo*
friend *amigo* (male); *amiga* (female)
sweetheart *novio* (male); *novia* (female)

son; daughter *hijo; hija*
brother; sister *hermano; hermana*
father; mother *padre; madre*
grandfather; grandmother *abuelo; abuela*

TRANSPORTATION

Where is...? *¿Dónde está...?*
How far is it to...? *¿A cuánto está...?*
from... to... *de... a...*
How many blocks? *¿Cuántas cuadras?*
Where (Which) is the way to...? *¿Dónde está el camino a...?*
the bus station *la terminal de autobuses*
the bus stop *la parada de autobuses*
Where is this bus going? *¿Adónde va este autobús?*
the taxi stand *la parada de taxis*
the train station *la estación de ferrocarril*
the boat *el barco*
the launch *lancha; tiburonera*
the dock *el muelle*
the airport *el aeropuerto*
I'd like a ticket to... *Quisiera un boleto a...*
first (second) class *primera (segunda) clase*
roundtrip *ida y vuelta*
reservation *reservación*
baggage *equipaje*
Stop here, please. *Pare aquí, por favor.*
the entrance *la entrada*
the exit *la salida*
the ticket office *la oficina de boletos*
(very) near; far *(muy) cerca; lejos*
to; toward *a*
by; through *por*
from *de*
the right *la derecha*
the left *la izquierda*
straight ahead *derecho; directo*
in front *en frente*
beside *al lado*
behind *atrás*
the corner *la esquina*
the stoplight *la semáforo*
a turn *una vuelta*

right here *aquí*
somewhere around here *por acá*
right there *allí*
somewhere around there *por allá*
road *el camino*
street; boulevard *calle; bulevar*
block *la cuadra*
highway *carretera*
kilometer *kilómetro*
bridge; toll *puente; cuota*
address *dirección*
north; south *norte; sur*
east; west *oriente (este); poniente (oeste)*

ACCOMMODATIONS

hotel *hotel*
Is there a room? *¿Hay cuarto?*
May I (may we) see it? *¿Puedo (podemos) verlo?*
What is the rate? *¿Cuál es el precio?*
Is that your best rate? *¿Es su mejor precio?*
Is there something cheaper? *¿Hay algo más económico?*
a single room *un cuarto sencillo*
a double room *un cuarto doble*
double bed *cama matrimonial*
twin beds *camas gemelas*
with private bath *con baño*
hot water *agua caliente*
shower *ducha*
towels *toallas*
soap *jabón*
toilet paper *papel higiénico*
blanket *frazada; manta*
sheets *sábanas*
air-conditioned *aire acondicionado*
fan *abanico; ventilador*
key *llave*
manager *gerente*

FOOD

I'm hungry *Tengo hambre.*
I'm thirsty. *Tengo sed.*
menu *carta; menú*

order *orden*
glass *vaso*
fork *tenedor*
knife *cuchillo*
spoon *cuchara*
napkin *servilleta*
soft drink *refresco*
coffee *café*
tea *té*
drinking water *agua pura; agua potable*
bottled carbonated water *agua mineral*
bottled uncarbonated water *agua sin gas*
beer *cerveza*
wine *vino*
milk *leche*
juice *jugo*
cream *crema*
sugar *azúcar*
cheese *queso*
snack *antojo; botana*
breakfast *desayuno*
lunch *almuerzo*
daily lunch special *comida corrida (or el menú del día depending on region)*
dinner *comida (often eaten in late afternoon); cena (a late-night snack)*
the check *la cuenta*
eggs *huevos*
bread *pan*
salad *ensalada*
fruit *fruta*
mango *mango*
watermelon *sandía*
papaya *papaya*
banana *plátano*
apple *manzana*
orange *naranja*
lime *limón*
fish *pescado*
shellfish *mariscos*
shrimp *camarones*
meat (without) *(sin) carne*
chicken *pollo*
pork *puerco*

beef; steak *res; bistec*
bacon; ham *tocino; jamón*
fried *frito*
roasted *asada*
barbecue; barbecued *barbacoa; al carbón*

SHOPPING

money *dinero*
money-exchange bureau *casa de cambio*
I would like to exchange traveler's
  checks. *Quisiera cambiar cheques de
  viajero.*
What is the exchange rate? *¿Cuál es el tipo
  de cambio?*
How much is the commission? *¿Cuánto
  cuesta la comisión?*
Do you accept credit cards? *¿Aceptan
  tarjetas de crédito?*
money order *giro*
How much does it cost? *¿Cuánto cuesta?*
What is your final price? *¿Cuál es su último
  precio?*
expensive *caro*
cheap *barato; económico*
more *más*
less *menos*
a little *un poco*
too much *demasiado*

HEALTH

Help me please. *Ayúdeme por favor.*
I am ill. *Estoy enfermo.*
Call a doctor. *Llame un doctor.*
Take me to... *Lléveme a...*
hospital *hospital; sanatorio*
drugstore *farmacia*
pain *dolor*
fever *fiebre*
headache *dolor de cabeza*
stomach ache *dolor de estómago*
burn *quemadura*
cramp *calambre*
nausea *náusea*
vomiting *vomitar*

medicine *medicina*
antibiotic *antibiótico*
pill; tablet *pastilla*
aspirin *aspirina*
ointment; cream *pomada; crema*
bandage *venda*
cotton *algodón*
sanitary napkins use brand name, e.g., Kotex
birth control pills *pastillas anticonceptivas*
contraceptive foam *espuma anticonceptiva*
condoms *preservativos; condones*
toothbrush *cepilla dental*
dental floss *hilo dental*
toothpaste *crema dental*
dentist *dentista*
toothache *dolor de muelas*

POST OFFICE AND COMMUNICATIONS

long-distance telephone *teléfono larga
  distancia*
I would like to call... *Quisiera llamar a...*
collect *por cobrar*
station to station *a quien contesta*
person to person *persona a persona*
credit card *tarjeta de crédito*
post office *correo*
general delivery *lista de correo*
letter *carta*
stamp *estampilla, timbre*
postcard *tarjeta*
aerogram *aerograma*
air mail *correo aereo*
registered *registrado*
money order *giro*
package; box *paquete; caja*
string; tape *cuerda; cinta*

AT THE BORDER

border *frontera*
customs *aduana*
immigration *migración*
tourist card *tarjeta de turista*
inspection *inspección; revisión*

passport *pasaporte*
profession *profesión*
marital status *estado civil*
single *soltero*
married; divorced *casado; divorciado*
widowed *viudado*
insurance *seguros*
title *título*
driver's license *licencia de manejar*

AT THE GAS STATION

gas station *gasolinera*
gasoline *gasolina*
unleaded *sin plomo*
full, please *lleno, por favor*
tire *llanta*
tire repair shop *vulcanizadora*
air *aire*
water *agua*
oil (change) *aceite (cambio)*
grease *grasa*
My... doesn't work. *Mi... no sirve.*
battery *batería*
radiator *radiador*
alternator *alternador*
generator *generador*
tow truck *grúa*
repair shop *taller mecánico*
tune-up *afinación*
auto parts store *refaccionería*

VERBS

Verbs are the key to getting along in Spanish. They employ mostly predictable forms and come in three classes, which end in *ar*, *er*, and *ir*, respectively:

to buy *comprar*
I buy, you (he, she, it) buys *compro, compra*
we buy, you (they) buy *compramos, compran*

to eat *comer*
I eat, you (he, she, it) eats *como, come*
we eat, you (they) eat *comemos, comen*

to climb *subir*
I climb, you (he, she, it) climbs *subo, sube*
we climb, you (they) climb *subimos, suben*

Here are more (with irregularities indicated):

to do or make *hacer* (regular except for *hago*, I do or make)
to go *ir* (very irregular: *voy, va, vamos, van*)
to go (walk) *andar*
to love *amar*
to work *trabajar*
to want *desear, querer*
to need *necesitar*
to read *leer*
to write *escribir*
to repair *reparar*
to stop *parar*
to get off (the bus) *bajar*
to arrive *llegar*
to stay (remain) *quedar*
to stay (lodge) *hospedar*
to leave *salir* (regular except for *salgo*, I leave)
to look at *mirar*
to look for *buscar*
to give *dar* (regular except for *doy*, I give)
to carry *llevar*
to have *tener* (irregular but important: *tengo, tiene, tenemos, tienen*)
to come *venir* (similarly irregular: *vengo, viene, venimos, vienen*)

Spanish has two forms of "to be":

to be *estar* (regular except for *estoy*, I am)
to be *ser* (very irregular: *soy, es, somos, son*)

Use *estar* when speaking of location or a temporary state of being: "I am at home." "*Estoy en casa.*" "I'm sick." "*Estoy enfermo.*" Use *ser* for a permanent state of being: "I am a doctor." "*Soy doctora.*"

NUMBERS

zero *cero*
one *uno*
two *dos*
three *tres*
four *cuatro*
five *cinco*
six *seis*
seven *siete*
eight *ocho*
nine *nueve*
10 *diez*
11 *once*
12 *doce*
13 *trece*
14 *catorce*
15 *quince*
16 *dieciseis*
17 *diecisiete*
18 *dieciocho*
19 *diecinueve*
20 *veinte*
21 *veinte y uno* or *veintiuno*
30 *treinta*
40 *cuarenta*
50 *cincuenta*
60 *sesenta*
70 *setenta*
80 *ochenta*
90 *noventa*
100 *ciento*
101 *ciento y uno* or *cientiuno*
200 *doscientos*
500 *quinientos*
1,000 *mil*
10,000 *diez mil*
100,000 *cien mil*
1,000,000 *millón*
one half *medio*
one third *un tercio*
one fourth *un cuarto*

TIME

What time is it? *¿Qué hora es?*
It's one o'clock. *Es la una.*
It's three in the afternoon. *Son las tres de la tarde.*
It's 4 a.m. *Son las cuatro de la mañana.*
six-thirty *seis y media*
a quarter till eleven *un cuarto para las once*
a quarter past five *las cinco y cuarto*
an hour *una hora*

DAYS AND MONTHS

Monday *lunes*
Tuesday *martes*
Wednesday *miércoles*
Thursday *jueves*
Friday *viernes*
Saturday *sábado*
Sunday *domingo*
today *hoy*
tomorrow *mañana*
yesterday *ayer*
January *enero*
February *febrero*
March *marzo*
April *abril*
May *mayo*
June *junio*
July *julio*
August *agosto*
September *septiembre*
October *octubre*
November *noviembre*
December *diciembre*
a week *una semana*
a month *un mes*
after *después*
before *antes*

(Courtesy of Bruce Whipperman, author of *Moon Pacific Mexico*.)

Suggested Reading

The titles below are all available on Amazon. com, either new or used in the case of many that are out of print. In Ecuador, the Libri Mundi bookstore in Quito and Guayaquil is your best bet, or try The English Bookshop (Calama and Diego de Almagro, Mariscal Sucre) in Quito.

Angermeyer, Johanna. *My Father's Island: A Galápagos Quest.* New York: Viking, 1990. Out of print. Life in the Galápagos through much of the 20th century.

Bassett, Carol Ann. *Galapagos at the Crossroads: Pirates, Biologists, Tourists and Creationists Battle for Darwin's Cradle of Evolution.* Washington DC: National Geographic, 2009. Provocative analysis of the islands' environmental problems.

Castro, Isabel. *A Guide to the Birds of the Galápagos Islands.* Princeton, NJ: Princeton University Press, 1996. Presents every species to have been recorded within the archipelago, including accidentals and vagrants; 32 color plates.

Darwin, Charles. *The Origin of Species by Means of Natural Selection.* New York: Signet Classics, 2003. The book that shook the world—and, as a bonus, it's one of the few groundbreaking scientific works that's truly readable.

Darwin, Charles. *The Voyage of the Beagle.* New York: Penguin USA, 1999. A classic of early travel literature written by a wide-eyed, brilliant young man setting out to see the whole world. You can almost witness his theories being born.

Darwin, Charles, and Mark Ridley, ed. *The Darwin Reader.* New York: W. W. Norton & Co., 1996. Selections from Darwin's works, including *The Voyage of the Beagle* and *The Origin of Species.*

De Roy, Tui. *Spectacular Galápagos: Exploring an Extraordinary World.* Westport, CT: Hugh Lauter Levin, 1999. Text and breathtaking photographs by one of the islands' foremost advocates. De Roy lived in the Galápagos for 35 years and also wrote *Galápagos: Islands Born of Fire* (Lexington, KY: Warwick Publications, 2000).

Jackson, Michael. *Galápagos: A Natural History.* Calgary: University of Calgary Press, 1994. This definitive guide to the islands is a must-read for every visitor.

McMullen, Conley. *Flowering Plants of the Galápagos.* Ithaca, NY: Cornell University Press, 1999.

Weiner, Jonathan. *The Beak of the Finch: A Story of Evolution in Our Own Time.* New York: Vintage Books, 1995. Describes the work of Rosemary and Peter Grant, who have studied 20 generations of finches on Daphne Major over two decades.

Wittmer, Margaret. *Floreana: A Woman's Pilgrimage to the Galápagos.* Wakefield, RI: Moyer Bell, 1990. First-hand account of early Floreana settlers, including Margaret's account of the mysterious events of the 1930s.

Internet Resources

GALÁPAGOS WEBSITES

Galápagos National Park
www.galapagospark.org
Comprehensive website with news and descriptions of visitor sites.

Charles Darwin Foundation
www.darwinfoundation.org
News about the foundation's research and volunteer opportunities.

Galápagos Conservation Trust
www.savegalapagos.org
UK-based charity that funds conservation projects on the archipelago.

Conservation International
www.conservation.org
U.S. charity with a strong presence on the Galápagos.

International Galápagos Tour Operators Association
www.igtoa.org
List of accredited tour operators and nonprofit organizations.

ECUADOR TRAVEL AND TOURISM

Ecuador's Ministry of Tourism website
http://ecuador.travel
Complete online guide.

Quito Official Travel Information
www.quito.com.ec
City tourism office's website, with comprehensive information.

Visita Guayaquil
www.visitaguayaquil.com
Online guide to Guayaquil in 13 languages, including English and Spanish.

GOVERNMENT

U.S. Department of State Ecuador Country Profile
http://travel.state.gov
Click on "Ecuador" in the country menu.

British Foreign Office Travel Advice
www.fco.gov.uk/en/travel-and-living-abroad/
Click on "Ecuador" in the country menu.

Ecuadorian Embassy in Washington DC
www.ecuador.org
Up-to-date information on visas and immigration issues, in English.

Ecuador's Ministry of External Relations
www.mmrree.gob.ec
Up-to-date information on visas and immigration issues, in Spanish.

Presidency of Ecuador
www.presidencia.gov.ec
The latest news and views from Ecuador's government.

U.S. Embassy in Ecuador
www.usembassy.org.ec

WEATHER AND THE NATURAL WORLD

Weather.com
www.weather.com
Five- and 10-day forecasts throughout Ecuador.

**Instituto Geofísico-Escuela
Politécnica Nacional**
www.igepn.edu.ec
Local volcano watchers provide daily updates, seismograms within 15 minutes of events, and photos.

NEWS AND MEDIA

El Comercio **online**
www.elcomercio.com
Quito-based national daily newspaper, in Spanish.

El Universo **online**
www.eluniverso.com
Guayaquil-based national daily newspaper, in Spanish.

Hoy **online**
www.hoy.com.ec
Quito-based national daily newspaper, in Spanish.

LANGUAGE

SpanishDICT.com
www.spanishdict.com
Online Spanish dictionary.

Learn Spanish
www.studyspanish.com
Free, award-winning online tutorial.

Index

List of Maps

Acknowledgments

I would like to thank many friends and colleagues in Ecuador and the Galapagos who gave their time, local knowledge, expertise and photography to this project: Chris O'Connell, Esteban Velásquez at Via Natura, Dominic Hamilton at Metropolitan Touring, and the staff at the Finch Bay Eco Hotel. I'd particularly like to thank University Especialidades Espiritu Santo (UEES) for giving me the time to complete this project.

Thanks to all at Avalon Travel, in particular Grace Fujimoto for commissioning me, to Erin Raber for her advice and guidance as editor, to Domini Dragoone for sourcing excellent photography, and to Mike Morgenfeld for his work on the maps.

Most importantly, I'd like to thank my family: my parents for the education and my children Jake and Isabella for keeping me smiling. Special thanks to my wife Carolina, who always supports me and who has been through a lot in the past year. Her bravery and strength are my biggest inspiration.

www.moon.com

MOON.COM is ready to help plan your next trip! Filled with fresh trip ideas and strategies, author interviews, informative travel blogs, a detailed map library, and descriptions of all the Moon guidebooks, Moon.com is all you need to get out and explore the world—or even places in your own backyard. While at Moon.com, sign up for our monthly e-newsletter for updates on new releases, travel tips, and expert advice from our on-the-go Moon authors. As always, when you travel with Moon, expect an experience that is uncommon and truly unique.

KEEP UP WITH MOON ON FACEBOOK AND TWITTER
JOIN THE MOON PHOTO GROUP ON FLICKR

MAP SYMBOLS

≡≡≡	Expressway	【	Highlight	✗	Airfield	⌕	Golf Course
≡≡≡	Primary Road	○	City/Town	✈	Airport	🅿	Parking Area
≡≡≡	Secondary Road	◉	State Capital	▲	Mountain	≜	Archaeological Site
▫▫▫	Unpaved Road	⊛	National Capital	✛	Unique Natural Feature	♠	Church
-------	Trail	★	Point of Interest			🛢	Gas Station
···········	Ferry	•	Accommodation	⟆	Waterfall	⬭	Glacier
⤳⤳	Railroad	▼	Restaurant/Bar	▲	Park	⬭	Mangrove
≡≡≡	Pedestrian Walkway	▪	Other Location	▣	Trailhead	▨	Reef
▥▥▥	Stairs	Λ	Campground	⛷	Skiing Area	▱	Swamp

CONVERSION TABLES

°C = (°F - 32) / 1.8
°F = (°C x 1.8) + 32
1 inch = 2.54 centimeters (cm)
1 foot = 0.304 meters (m)
1 yard = 0.914 meters
1 mile = 1.6093 kilometers (km)
1 km = 0.6214 miles
1 fathom = 1.8288 m
1 chain = 20.1168 m
1 furlong = 201.168 m
1 acre = 0.4047 hectares
1 sq km = 100 hectares
1 sq mile = 2.59 square km
1 ounce = 28.35 grams
1 pound = 0.4536 kilograms
1 short ton = 0.90718 metric ton
1 short ton = 2,000 pounds
1 long ton = 1.016 metric tons
1 long ton = 2,240 pounds
1 metric ton = 1,000 kilograms
1 quart = 0.94635 liters
1 US gallon = 3.7854 liters
1 Imperial gallon = 4.5459 liters
1 nautical mile = 1.852 km

°FAHRENHEIT   °CELSIUS

°FAHRENHEIT	°CELSIUS	
230	110	
220		
210	100	WATER BOILS
200		
190	90	
180	80	
170		
160	70	
150		
140	60	
130		
120	50	
110		
100	40	
90	30	
80		
70	20	
60		
50	10	
40		
30	0	WATER FREEZES
20	-10	
10		
0	-20	
-10		
-20	-30	
-30		
-40	-40	

Clock face numerals: 12 24, 1 13, 2 14, 3 15, 4 16, 5 17, 6 18, 7 19, 8 20, 9 21, 10 22, 11 23

INCH 0 1 2 3 4

CM 0 1 2 3 4 5 6 7 8 9 10

MOON GALÁPAGOS ISLANDS

Avalon Travel
a member of the Perseus Books Group
1700 Fourth Street
Berkeley, CA 94710, USA
www.moon.com

Editor: Erin Raber
Series Manager: Kathryn Ettinger
Copy Editor: Christopher Church
Graphics and Production Coordinator: Domini Dragoone
Cover Designer: Domini Dragoone
Map Editor: Mike Morgenfeld
Cartographers: Chris Henrick and Kaitlin Jaffe
Indexer: Greg Jewett

ISBN-13: 978-1-59880-975-6
ISSN: 2169-8201

Printing History
1st Edition — November 2012
5 4 3

Front cover photo: © Eric Rorer/Aurora Photos. Giant tortoises walk along the floor of Alcedo Volcano on Isabela Island.
Title page photo: © Liudmila Komolova/123rf. Submerged volcanic crater with Pinnacle Rock in the background, Bartolomé.
Front color photos: pgs. 4, 8 (left), 9 (right), and 23 © Michael Zysman/123rf; pgs. 5 (top left) and 29 © Leonid Spektor/123rf; pgs. 5 (top right) and 7 (top) © Justin Black/123rf; pg. 5 (bottom) © Sergei Uriadnikov; pgs. 6 (top left), 21 (right), 26, and 28 (right) © Javarman Javarman/123rf; pgs. 6 (top right and bottom) and 30 (both photos) © Kjersti Jorgensen/123rf; pg. 7 (bottom) © Robert Ranson/123rf; pg. 8 (right) © Morten Elm/123rf; pg. 9 (left) © Stefan Ember/123rf; pg. 10 © DesignPics/123rf; pg. 11 © Matt Ragen/123rf; pg. 12 © Ramiro Salazar; pgs. 14 and 17 (top) © Chris O'Connell; pg. 15 © Daniel Alvarez/123rf; pg. 16 © Alvaro Sevilla Design/Wikimedia Commons*; pg. 17 (bottom) © Terrance Phillips/123rf; pg. 18 © Nick Bell/123rf; pg. 19 © Ben Westwood; pg. 20 © Erkki Tamsalu/123rf; pg. 21 (left) © Leighton O'Connor/123rf; pg. 22 © Dieder Brandelet/123rf; pg. 24 © Thomas Sztanek/123rf; pg. 25 © Jens Klingebiel/123rf; pg. 27 © Ammit Pie/123rf; pgs. 28 (left) and 32 © Siete Bravo/123rf; pg. 31 © Rein Ketelaars (http://www.flickr.com/photos/67396014@N00) from Nijmegen, Netherlands*.

Printed in Canada by Friesens

KEEPING CURRENT

If you have a favorite gem you'd like to see included in the next edition, or see anything that needs updating, clarification, or correction, please drop us a line. Send your comments via email to feedback@moon.com, or use the address above.